Columbia Books of Architecture
Catalogue 3

THE INTERNATIONAL STYLE: EXHIBITION 15 AND THE MUSEUM OF MODERN ART

by Terence Riley
edited/designed by Stephen Perrella

RIZZOLI/*cba*
NEW YORK

The International Style: Exhibition 15 and The Museum of Modern Art
was produced at Columbia University Graduate School of Architecture, Planning and Preservation, Avery Hall 403, New York, New York 10027, and published on the occasion of an exhibition at the Arthur Ross Architectural Gallery, Buell Hall, from March 9 to May 2, 1992.

Bernard Tschumi *Dean*
Terence Riley *Curator of Exhibition*
Joan Ockman *Director of Publications*
Stephen Perrella *Editor/Graphic Designer*
Joseph Rosa *Director of Exhibition*
Edward Eigen *Research Assistant*

First published in the Unites States of America in 1992 by
Rizzoli International Publications, Inc.
300 Park Avenue South
New York, New York 10010

Printed in the United States

Contents

Henry-Russell Hitchcock, 1937.

Foreword

Philip Johnson

It is just 60 years since the exhibition "Modern Architecture" was opened at The Museum of Modern Art. Three of us gave birth. Alfred Barr, Russell Hitchcock and myself. I was Director. Since I am the only living member of the triumvirate, my memory of the event *should* be the determining factor in any discussion of the revival of the show. But "history is written by the victors" they say. In this case, the new history is written by the "victors" of the next generation. Terence Riley, almost 50 years my junior has supplanted in this document my memories as the "true" story of the early days at the Museum. How skewed my memory is! And naturally in my favor.

It is good to have it straight, to have my mistakes so boldly pointed out and some of my more petty victories, my judgments of 1930–1931, reconfirmed.

It is clear now that the theory and scholarship were by Hitchcock, the inspiration and drive were by Alfred Barr. I did the leg work, made all the mistakes and prophesied a few of the prophecies that now seem prescient: Mies van der Rohe, Le Corbusier, J.J.P. Oud and Gropius are still triumphantly important. The International Style, as we dubbed the movement which lasted at least a generation or two, is still dimly around.

The history of the architectural beginnings in the twenties and thirties is a fascinating story. Terence Riley's account of our 1932 stand proves to be one very important punctuation point.

Preface

Bernard Tschumi

This catalogue is published on the occasion of an exhibition at the Columbia University architecture galleries recreating—sixty years later—the "Modern Architecture—International Exhibition" at The Museum of Modern Art in New York.

To reconstruct in a university context a historical event that first took place in a museum would be mere scholarly documentation were it not symptomatic of a series of inversions that characterize architecture today.

Modern Architecture—International Exhibition. The Museum of Modern Art, February 10–March 23, 1932. Installation of Le Corbusier's exhibit

The first inversion has been noted by others. It is the inversion of the direction of influence between education and practice. Just as the 1932 exhibition found its source material in the practice of its time, so schools of architecture formerly found their models in the profession. The avant-garde of architecture did not reside in the schools. Witness Columbia in 1932: its conservative Beaux-Arts curriculum lasted well into the late thirties.

Today the line of influence has been reversed. The profession (and sometimes the museums) now look to the schools for fresh ideas. As corporate practice in America continues to relish the Beaux-Arts historicism introduced in the seventies, the schools, from the Architectural Association in London to Cooper Union and Columbia in New York, often wish to propagate the idea of a new avant-garde.

That school production has an influence on built practice suggests a second inversion. In the period illustrated in the 1932 exhibition far more was built in the United States than in European countries suffering from sluggish economies. Yet most of the architectural ideas and images originated in Europe. Sixty years later, the reverse is true: America has entered a serious building recession while Europe has seen an unusual burst of building energy. Yet rarely has America been so fertile a ground for architectural theory, often outdistancing European architectural thought.

Other inversions are worth noting. Today the word *style* is discredited by all except critics attempting to reduce serious research by young architects through derogatory labels ("decon," "neo-modernism"), unfairly ignoring the social and programmatic concerns that often underlie contemporary experimentation. Today the obsolete notion of fixed, identifiable styles is increasingly replaced by ever changing and self-challenging conceptual devices.

It is striking that these contemporary devices sometimes recall two aspects of the early 20th century avant-garde that the 1932 International Style exhibition superbly ignored: namely, the forces of futurism, constructivism, dada and surrealism on one hand and of advanced technology on the other, from the tensile structures of the twenties to today's computer-generated images. These are the very sources which, together with literary parallels, have been most revered by today's architectural inventors.

A final note on the word *international*. As we may hope today that the idea of nationalities and nationalism will become a thing of the past, long before World War II and the Cold War the title of the 1932 exhibition showed great revolutionary insight. Too bad that insight was later narrowed to a "style."

Alfred H. Barr, Jr., Philip Johnson and Martha Barr. Cortona, Italy, 1932.

THE INTERNATIONAL STYLE:
EXHIBITION 15 AND
THE MUSEUM OF MODERN ART

Terence Riley

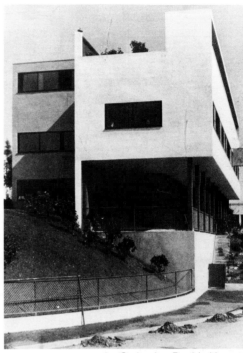

Le Corbusier, Double House,
Weissenhofsiedlung, Stuttgart,1927.
View from street

The purpose of this essay is twofold: to document the international exhibition of modern architecture held at the Museum of Modern Art in New York in 1932 and to trace the exhibition's curatorial development.

Although Exhibition 15 (as it is recorded in the museum's archives) has figured prominently in the development of architectural theory and practice in the twentieth century, no accurate visual record of the event exists. Of the fifty-eight architectural images (exclusive of plans) reproduced in the catalogue[1] less than half actually appeared in the exhibition. Nearly seventy photographs in the exhibition were not included in the catalogue. None of the photographs of work by J.J.P. Oud in the catalogue were in the exhibition.

In addition to a great number of omissions, the curators frequently represented the same project with different images in the catalogue and in the exhibition respectively. Not all were not substantially different (see 119 & upper right this page), but many discrepancies were egregious, particularly since so many projects were represented by a single photograph. For example, Le Corbusier's Villa Stein was presented in the exhibition by a photograph of the garden façade; in the catalogue an oblique view of the entry façade was substituted (see 117 & lower right this page). The catalogue complemented rather than documented the exhibition. In the curators' own words the purpose of the catalogue was "to explain the aims and achievements of the greatest contemporary architects"[2]—a significantly greater ambition than merely documenting the exhibition. Ironically, the catalogue and, to some extent, the book *The International Style*,[3] published at the time of the exhibition, have supplanted the actual historical event.

Le Corbusier, Villa Stein at Garches, 1928.
Entry façade

The financial vicissitudes of the Depression, which plagued the entire curatorial process, exacerbated the discrepancies between exhibition and catalogue. An

9

Frank Lloyd Wright, Ocatilla Camp, Chandler, Arizona, 1929. Construction photo

early budget for the project indicates that the curators had originally hoped to produce a "large catalogue" to document the work of the prominent architects, "reports" to document the technical exhibits (which included the section on housing) and a "guide" to the exhibition. The last was never printed, and rather late in the process the large catalogue and the reports were combined and a great number of projects added without illustrations.[4] The editorial process continued up to the last minute and the catalogue barely made it into print at all, going to press a scant three weeks before the exhibition opening.[5]

The account of the exhibition's curatorial development is no more comprehensive. Neither the curators[6] Henry-Russell Hitchcock (1903–1987) and Philip Johnson (b. 1906) nor museum director Alfred H. Barr Jr. (1902–1981) have ever written at length about the process. As a result, a number of unsupported anecdotes have grown up around the exhibition, many of them appearing in print. The research for this essay consisted of studying more than 2500 documents in the various archives at The Museum of Modern Art, New York, as well as other primary and secondary sources to reconstruct the curatorial process and the actual installation. While the documents do not conclusively lay to rest all of the dubious anecdotes, they do clarify several important issues. For example, previously unexamined correspondence[7] shows that Hitchcock and Johnson conceived of the International Style project first as a book and some time later as an exhibition, despite their respective recollections to the contrary.

These and other issues surrounding the chronology of the exhibition's inception and planning (which occurred within a compressed eighteen-month time frame) seem to have slipped, not surprisingly, from the memories of those involved. Nor is it surprising that the final presentation of the project as an exhibition, catalogue and book has obscured the various intellectual positions taken during the planning phase. From a historical point of view, the curators' original proposals, which included exhibiting an ideal factory prototype and work by Norman Bel Geddes but not by Richard Neutra, add considerably to our understanding of the actual event.

While critics' and historians' opinions of the merits of the International Style vary widely, the importance of Exhibition 15 in relation to the subsequent history of American architecture is rarely disputed. The substantive effects of the exhibition are many: the introduction of the European architectural avant-garde, particularly Mies van der Rohe, to America; the increased visibility and acceptance of modernist architects before the Second World War; and the postwar emergence of the "Harvard School" under the leadership of Walter Gropius.[8]

The purpose of this research then, is first and foremost documentary to look more closely at the event, its planning and the circumstances surrounding it in order to understand more fully what actually transpired. A secondary goal may also be realized though it is necessarily beyond the scope of this essay. If the development and planning of Exhibition 15 are now only dimly known, the critical history of the event must also be considered incomplete. As the International Style has come to be near analogous to the history of modernism in America, it is hoped that this essay may contribute to a broader, critical reevaluation of the event and its subsequent transformations over the past sixty years.

Mies van der Rohe.

Walter Gropius.

Part One: Summer 1930

Rarely can the genesis of an idea be determined with any certainty, particularly with regard to events long past. But it can be said that the project which was to become Exhibition 15 was initiated 18 June 1930. Two days later Johnson writes from Europe:

> But the book. I cannot put it off any longer although we just got the idea [the] day before yesterday. It had been in mind for a year as you know, but I really didn't want to take the risk of alone carrying through such an ambitious plan when I knew so little about architecture really. And Russell has had the idea because he realized that his book was badly illustrated. So what the plan is now is to rewrite in a more popular way paying close attention to the buildings illustrated, parts of his book and incorporate about 150 full page half-tones. The text will be first and then the pictures in a bunch. Of course one disadvantage perhaps will be that the book will be in German. . . . The text will practically be a translation of Russell's big book.[1]

Hitchcock's decision to recommence the work of his just published book is curious. In letters to Lewis Mumford preceding his and Johnson's 1930 trip through Europe, Hitchcock professes both a weariness with the subject and a plan to begin work on a book on "Romantic architecture . . . from 1750–1850."[2] The decision to rewrite *Modern Architecture* "in a more popular way" with more illustrations was not, however, wholly spontaneous or inexplicable. Just before Hitchcock and Johnson sailed for Europe that summer Barr's review of Hitchcock's book was published in *The Hound and Horn*.[3] Barr is generally enthusiastic, describing the book as "a scholarly and critical achievement of the greatest originality and distinction." Even so, his objections are pointed. He criticizes Hitchcock's writing style saying, "his method and ideology seem too erudite for the ordinary reader." He also refers to the illustrated section as "parsimonious."

Johnson's letter was posted from the Hague and dated 20 June 1930, just weeks after he graduated *cum laude* from Harvard College at the age of twenty-three with a degree in philosophy. A year earlier Johnson had attended the graduation of his sister Theodate from Wellesley College, where he met the twenty-seven-year-old Barr,[4] who was teaching a course on modern art. In a month's time Barr would be interviewed by Abby Aldrich Rockefeller for the position of director of the Museum of Modern Art, set to open its first galleries later that year. Johnson became a frequent visitor to New York and a member of the museum's Junior Advisory Committee. Within the circle of young academics and aesthetes that Barr drew around the museum was Hitchcock, who like most of the group was a recent Harvard graduate.[5] A brilliant young art historian, Hitchcock graduated *magna cum laude* in 1924 after having completed his undergraduate studies in three years and spending his senior year studying architecture. He continued his graduate studies at Harvard and received his master's degree in 1927.[6] Hitchcock's friendship with Johnson began during this time.[7] After graduating, Johnson (with a Cord convertible in the cargo hold) sailed for Europe, meeting Hitchcock in Paris. The two then began an extended tour of the continent.

At the outset of the trip Johnson was admittedly the junior member of the duo. In his own words: "My relation to Russell in the business [of the book] is somewhat that of an apprentice, but I struggle hard, and with some success to keep my judgement independent."[8] While Johnson shows appropriate modesty concerning his relationship to Hitchcock, he was not unschooled in contemporary architecture. His "apprenticeship" thus far included familiarity with Hitchcock's writings (both *Modern Architecture* and his work on J.J.P. Oud) and Gustav Platz's *Die Baukunst der neuesten Zeit*;[9] previous trips to Europe, particularly the preceding summer when he visited the *Weissenhofsiedlung*; and the sophisticated discussions of Barr's circle.

J.J.P. Oud.

In subsequent letters throughout the summer Johnson repeatedly refers to the book. From Copenhagen in early July he writes:

> The book is coming along very well, though naturally Russell is doing the bigger share. I do the dirty work. But I am learning so much that I don't mind in the least. We won't see any publishers until we reach Berlin so naturally we don't know just what form it will take yet. I am terribly thrilled.[10]

Three days later Hitchcock and Johnson were in Hamburg, where they met Barr, who was traveling with J. B. Neumann, a dealer in modern art with a gallery on East 57th Street, and Cary Ross, a young poet and a member of the museum circle. Johnson relates that "Alfred is most enthusiastic" about the book. As the project was in a state of formulation, Barr's reaction was critical. Johnson writes, "The text is getting bigger and bigger in our minds but also more important. . . . [W]e are discussing subjects which lie much nearer to my heart than most of the old ones, such as new materials, construction, functionalism, and the fundamental aesthetic, especially of the style."[11]

Late August saw another important reference to the book: in explaining the difficulty in obtaining a German publisher Johnson comments, "No one wants another book on modern architecture here in Germany. . . . In vain do we explain that there has been no book covering the whole style and nothing but the style."[12] Lest there be any question of what exactly "the style" is, Otto Haesler, in responding to Johnson's request for photos, refers to "*das Buch— The New International Style 1922–1932.*"[13]

This transformation of the "old" book into a "more important" effort indicates that the broad outlines of the familiar arguments of *The International Style* were then under discussion. The focused aesthetic arguments of that book are foretold in Johnson's description of the book as being "about the style and nothing but the style."

By December 1930 the first written proposal for an exhibition of the "new architecture" was set down, yet the first draft of the book was not completed until some months later. In other words, for a time the book was an independent project and it can be assumed that, in whatever form it had developed, it greatly influenced the conception of the exhibition. The important question then is: How developed was the book prior to the conception of the exhibition?

With little other than Johnson's letters to document the events of the summer of 1930, the answer must be speculative and conditional. To this end it is useful to observe the fundamental restructuring in the "new" book of Hitchcock's previously published arguments. Like Platz, Hitchcock categorizes the architects in his initial international survey by nation (principally France, Holland and Germany). This organization is further reflected in Hitchcock's attempts to describe within a framework of nationalities the genealogies of the various avant-garde architects through their "new traditionalist"[14] predecessors. The latter are described positively and credited with breaking with the historic revivals of the nineteenth century.

In the new book this format changes radically. The "new traditionalists" are lowered in the author's esteem. Hitchcock writes: "Wright belongs to the international style no more than Behrens or Perret or Van de Velde. . . . They are more akin to the men of a hundred years ago than to the generation which has come to the fore since the War."[15] The term "new traditionalist" itself is dropped, and the work that it previously described is pejoratively characterized

Frank Lloyd Wright, circa 1931.

as "half-modern," "individualistic" and lacking in discipline.[16] Furthermore, the new book drops the national categories and views the avant-garde as being self-referential.

Hitchcock's restructuring of the historical landscape of *Modern Architecture* was indeed momentous though not wholly without precedent in his other writings or even within the old book itself: in the third section of *Modern Architecture* the author considers various names that might be "denotative for the work of the New Pioneers." Rejecting various appellations as insufficient, Hitchcock claims that "it is enough to call the architecture of the New Pioneers the *international style* of Le Corbusier, Oud and Gropius, of Lurçat, Rietveld and Mies van der Rohe."[17] A year earlier Hitchcock wrote of the work of Peter van der Meulen Smith: "He is the first . . . to develop an American version of what is very definitely not a French, nor a Dutch, nor a German, nor a Russian, but an *international style*."[18]

In place of the historiographic attitude of *Modern Architecture*, which embraces a succession of architects from the eighteenth century onward, the authors designate 1922 as the epiphanic moment when the new architecture, like Athena, springs from the heads of Le Corbusier, Oud, Mies and Gropius.[19] In addition to marking the beginning of the new "movement," the specific date further defined the gulf that now separated the "modern" from the "half-modern." Again, this restructuring was not wholly unprecedented. The year 1922 was mentioned as pivotal (albeit with little elaboration) in both *Modern Architecture* and Hitchcock's 1928 essay on Oud.[20]

However, a change in historical perspective alone need not have suggested a wholly different book. The change in voice is equally important, and in terms of its impact on the exhibition perhaps more important. Hitchcock's positive reaction to Barr's criticism of *Modern Architecture*'s writing style and illustrations is evident. Far more challenging, however, are Barr's rather lengthy comments regarding Hitchcock's critical attitude:

> *Even in praising Le Corbusier or condemning Ralph Adams Cram, his discriminating mildness is pervasive. But his caution in his last chapter,* The Architecture of the Future—1929, *is a little disappointing. At the end of the section on Romanticism he makes brilliant use of an essay by G. G. Scott upon exactly the same subject but published in 1857. Scott's pages are rich with enthusiasm. He dares greatly with true Victorian confidence and is as often right as wrong. By comparison Mr. Hitchcock's prophecies seem meager, dissipated by a rather conscious Spenglerian melancholy.*[21]

The museum director's public encouragement of Hitchcock to adopt more daring positions and forego his dispassionate demeanor was Barr's clarion call to join the fray. Barr's attempts to influence Hitchcock were not limited to the pages of *The Hound and Horn* but were integral to their collegial and personal interchange. If Barr found *Modern Architecture*'s vision of the future of architecture tinged with melancholy, Hitchcock's morbid speculation in his 1927 essay "The Decline of Architecture" is more so: "Architecture may shortly come to be pronounced dead. Yet even that is perhaps preferable to having the corpse continue, like Jeremy Bentham among us, attired like a superannuated prostitute in the finery of her various periods of youth and glory."[22] In this regard, the difference between *Modern Architecture* and *The International Style* that is to have most affect on the course of future events is the appearance in the latter of a proactive, critical edge in the authors' voice, aimed at promoting the "new architecture." Whereas the earlier book displays, as Barr notes, a

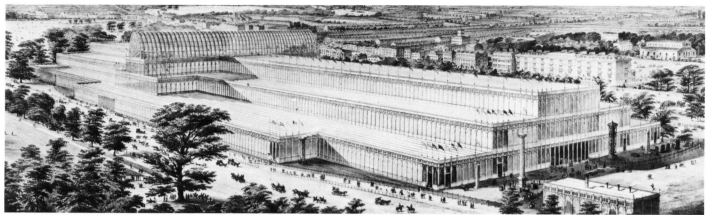

Joseph Paxton, Crystal Palace, London, 1851.
Aerial perspective

pronounced judiciousness with respect to contemporary architecture and its antecedents, *The International Style* makes few positive mentions of past architecture. Only the Crystal Palace and American architect H. H. Richardson escape the author's newfound enthusiasm.

Hitchcock and Johnson, with Barr's call to action ringing in their ears, crisscrossed Europe in June, July and August of 1930. Their excursion took them to France, Belgium, Holland, Germany, Sweden, Denmark and Switzerland, with Hitchcock continuing on to England and Johnson visiting Czechoslovakia and Austria. They not only saw most of the European projects represented in Exhibition 15 and *The International Style* but met many of the principal protagonists of the period, including Le Corbusier, Mies, Oud, Gropius, Otto Haesler and Sigfried Giedion. Johnson sums up the effect of their trip: "Russell and I find we have a tremendous advantage over everyone else in that we have seen more than everybody and that we have no national bias whatsoever."[23]

Whether, in retrospect, Hitchcock and Johnson had "no national bias" is arguable. Yet by the end of the summer of 1930 they had, indeed, seen more of the new architecture than any of their contemporaries and, despite their relative youth, were in a unique position among American architectural critics.

Part Two: Autumn 1930

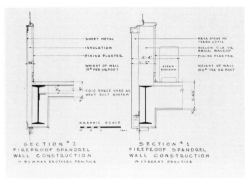

Bowman Brothers, Lake Front Building, 1930.
Construction analysis

During the autumn of 1930 Hitchcock, Johnson and Barr were back in the
United States: Hitchcock was teaching at Wellesley, and Barr was directing the
second season of exhibitions at The Museum of Modern Art. Johnson was in
the midst of renovating his East 52nd Street apartment according to a design
by Mies van der Rohe and frequently played host to Alfred and Marga
(Margaret Scolari) Barr, who lived in the same building, and Hitchcock. In
Marga Barr's words, "We were in and out of each others' apartments all the
time. Alfred and Philip talked incessantly about architecture."[1] Johnson was
also, presumably, working with Hitchcock on the preparation of *The
International Style* draft in addition to his first individual efforts in architectural
criticism: at the suggestion of J. B. Neumann he had become a corresponding
editor for *Die Form*, the publication of the Deutsche Werkbund.[2] In addition he
was working on what was to be one of his first published criticisms (rarely cited
in his bibliographies): a book review for the *New Republic* of Sheldon Cheney's
The New World Architecture.[3]

At some point after their return from Europe Barr, Hitchcock and Johnson
began discussing plans for Exhibition 15.[4] Although Barr had expressed
interest in mounting architectural exhibitions from the beginning of his tenure at
the museum, no documentation reveals specifically when the planning began or
who initiated the project and the curators' recollections are frequently
conflicting. Nonetheless, it is plausible that Barr suggested the idea based on
common discussions of the authors' experiences in Europe that summer
(see Notes for a more detailed discussion of the chronology of Exhibition 15,
page 89).

In early December a three-page memo by Johnson was submitted to museum
president A. Conger Goodyear describing an architectural exhibition (see
appendix 1) to be comprised of three sections: (1) models by the "most

Le Corbusier.

Raymond Hood,
Wallace Harrison and
L. Andrew Reinhard.

Shreve, Lamb & Harmon, Empire State Building,
NYC, 1931. Construction photo

prominent architects in the world"; (2) an "industrial" section; and (3) an international competition for young architects.

For the first section, nine architects were to be invited to submit models. With one exception[5] the proposed roster remained the same throughout the entire year of curatorial planning. From America were: Raymond Hood, Frank Lloyd Wright, Norman Bel Geddes, Howe & Lescaze and the Bowman Brothers; from Germany: Mies van der Rohe and Walter Gropius; from France: Le Corbusier; and from Holland: J.J.P. Oud.

Each of the architects was to build a model "of that type of building best suited to his genius." No mention is made of any additional material to be exhibited. Rather, it is proposed that the overview of each architect's work be presented in the "special catalogue." In addition to the "critical survey" of works the publication was to include biographical profiles and statements by the architects. The proposal's contention that "Hood may choose a skyscraper, Gropius an apartment house, Bel Geddes a theater" is slightly coy. No doubt a good deal of consideration was given to which type of project each architect would submit. A subsequent revision (in this essay the "February proposal") indicates that the curators intended to present projects, though it is clear that these were not to be utopian works but projections based on past works.

The Industrial section was to focus on three areas: an exhibit on large-scale urban construction, a presentation of an "advanced" factory prototype and an example of a "industrial housing project." As in the Modern Architects section, the three exhibits were to be presented in model form. Furthermore, the industrial projects were to be documented in "detailed reports," published separately from the catalogue, with plans and construction and cost information.

Interestingly, the proposal suggests that two of the technical exhibits would be "curated" by builders. The Starrett Bros. & Eken Co. is proposed to assemble the exhibit on urban construction. (A month prior to the submission of the December proposal Starrett Brothers completed the masonry and steel construction for the Empire State Building in a mere eleven months.) It is proposed that the Austin Company submit a prototype representing "the most advanced development of factory design." The housing exhibit, which is noted as being "of great significance" and described as "incorporating the most recent and scientific theory on the subject in America," was proposed without specifying who would lead the effort, although Johnson contacted the well-known architectural and social critic Lewis Mumford immediately after the project was approved.[6]

Like many components of the proposed exhibition, the international competition for "young architects" under thirty-five years of age is little elaborated. The suggested program is a school building—a problem of "universal interest." However, there is no indication of what proportion of the exhibition would be devoted to the competition entries, nor of how the substantial prize money (five thousand dollars—more than three times the median annual salary in 1929)[7] would be awarded.

Another important feature of the proposed exhibition, tentatively scheduled to open in February 1932, is described in even less detail: Mies is proposed as the exhibition designer. In the February proposal the design is better defined: "bases for the models, tables for the literature, chairs, photograph racks and partition screens of glass and metal."[8]

From the first proposal, then, Mies assumed a position of distinction above the other architects. In a 1982 interview with Peter Eisenman,[9] Johnson suggests

William Lescaze.

George Howe.

Mies van der Rohe, Tugendhat House, Brno,
Czechoslovakia, 1930. Interior view

Mies van der Rohe, Tugendhat House, Brno,
Czechoslovakia, 1930. View of stairwell

that he "fell in love" with Mies's work from his reading of Platz's *Die Baukunst der neuesten Zeit*, which he claimed occurred before he met Barr or Hitchcock in 1929. The 1927 edition of Platz includes four projects by Mies from the early 1920s, none of which were built: the brick and the concrete country houses, the concrete office building and the glass and steel apartment houses. Although not impossible, it seems unlikely that any neophyte (even one as precocious as Johnson) could have been so moved by the relatively modest reproductions of Mies's work in that volume.

If, in fact, Johnson had at that early date adopted a strong preference for Mies's work it would certainly have been a point of debate when Johnson joined the museum circle and grew close to Hitchcock and Barr. In *Modern Architecture* Hitchcock's estimation of Mies's work is certainly secondary to that of Gropius. He describes Mies as successful in his "technical experimentation" but decries the residual expressionism, as he saw it, in Mies's steel and glass towers.[10] Hitchcock is more positive about the Weissenhof apartments and Barcelona Pavilion (though he says curiously little about the latter) and ends his remarks with a cautious endorsement: Mies remains "primarily a man of promise."[11] Likewise, before Exhibition 15 Barr frequently cites Oud, Le Corbusier, and Gropius as the leaders of the new architecture, with no mention of Mies.

Before the opening of Exhibition 15 all three would change their estimation of Mies's work—the turning point appears to have been Johnson's photographs and descriptions of his visit to the Tugendhat House in August 1930, after which both Hitchcock and Barr added Mies to the previous triumvirate of new architects. Hitchcock also speaks more highly of the Barcelona project and refers to Mies as an "aesthetic innovator" rather than emphasizing his technical accomplishments.[12] While Johnson *may* have been taken originally with Mies's early projects he too adopted the position that they suffered from what he perceived to be a relationship to expressionism.[13]

Mies van der Rohe, German Pavilion, Barcelona, 1929.
View of Kolbe statue

Mies van der Rohe and Lilly Reich, Ruhtenberg
Apartment, Berlin, 1931.

In any event, Johnson was clearly impressed by his first encounter with Mies's built work: a number of apartment renovations in Berlin designed with Lilly Reich. Immediately afterward Johnson wrote to his mother seeking permission to hire Mies to redesign his New York apartment. His description of Mies's interior work ("elegant" and "simple")[14] is enthusiastic but pales next to his subsequent description, and instinctive rapport, with the design of the Tugendhat House:

> He has one room, very low ceilinged, one hundred feet long, toward the south all of glass from the ceiling to the very floor. Great sheets of plate glass that go into the floor electrically. The side of the room is at least thirty feet and is glass to the east. This room is divided into dining room, library and living room by partial walls which do not in the least destroy its size, but rather magnify it.[15]

Johnson's immediate appreciation of the house (in many ways different from the work to which he and Hitchcock had been exposed) confirmed his intentions to commission Mies. More eventful, though, was his meeting with the architect: "Mies is the greatest man that we or I have met. Oud I like better, I almost love Oud, such a dear man he is besides being a genius, but Mies is a great man."[16]

As outlined in the December proposal, the exhibition would be under the direction of a committee[17] consisting of Barr, Goodyear, Homer H. Johnson (Philip Johnson's father), Johnson (proposed committee secretary), Dr. G. F. Reber (a Swiss art collector whom Barr wanted to involve in the museum) and Mrs. John D. (Abby Aldrich) Rockefeller Jr. (who was also treasurer of the Board of Trustees and one of the museum founders). Alan R. Blackburn Jr., a schoolmate and close friend of Johnson, was proposed as the committee's executive secretary.

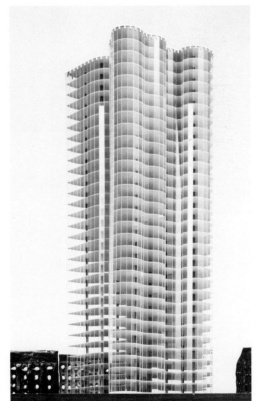

Mies van der Rohe, Glass Skyscraper, 1922.
Model

The proposal indicates financial concerns that were to plague the project from conception through installation. The proposed budget was enormous, especially in light of the worsening financial Depression. The December proposal hints at constraints on the museum: the curators insisted that funding for the exhibition could be raised outside of the museum (the entire budget of which at the time came from trustees' donations), specifically from "industrialists and builders."[18]

A one-page introduction outlines the "need for an exhibition of modern architecture." Half of the argument is devoted to a global survey of modern architectural "activity" citing, principally, the works of Wright, Neutra, Hood, Mart Stam, Mies, the Bauhaus and Le Corbusier. In contradistinction to this activity is the "chaos of conflicting and often unintelligent building" to be found in America.

The December proposal is the first in a series of proposals and revisions prepared for Goodyear, the trustees, industrialists, critics, potential donors and "subscribers."[19] The texts change slightly from proposal to proposal, edited to suit each particular audience. As such they are more interesting for their promotional than intellectual content. The central proposition changes little, however: a new architecture, characterized by an "integral and decidedly rational mode of building," is being developed by "a progressive group of architects" in Europe, America and throughout the world. The timely support of this movement, in the minds of the curators, will provide a model for reforming the unenlightened conservatives of America's entrenched construction industry and architectural profession.

It is useful to compare the December proposal with *The International Style*, then in progress, or at least to the book's broad outlines as suggested by Johnson's letters. In both, the frame of reference is an aesthetic theory with, at best, vague references to social or political concerns. The proposal makes plain that the proposed architects were "chosen as representing the highest *aesthetic* achievements in architecture." Social, economic and technical concerns are referred to obliquely (more prominently in the proposal than in the book but in both separately and secondarily). The basis of Hitchcock and Johnson's aesthetic position is artifact-oriented connoisseurship. From the book: "Architecture is always a set of actual monuments, not a vague corpus of theory."[20] In this spirit, it is no surprise that the proposed architects (though of disparate ideological orientations) had reputations, with the exception of Bel Geddes, based on executed commissions.[21] The proposed exhibition format contributes to the curators' artifact-based attitude: the scale models, themselves tangible *objets*, are surrogates for the actual monuments, as space limitations, "of course, prevent the display of any full-sized work of architecture."[22] The proposal even suggests that the models could become part of the museum's collection.

The book's somewhat truncated historiography is also implicit in the structure of the proposed exhibition. With the exception of Wright, the work of the "new traditionalists" counts for naught, even background. The omission was not unnoticed: Catherine Bauer, the author of *Modern Housing* and an associate of Mumford, reports: "I sweetly suggested in a letter that [Johnson] give a section to the history of modern architecture, so that no one would think it was invented by Norman Bel Geddes and the Bowman Brothers . . . the day before yesterday."[23]

The inclusion of an industrial section reflects a sentiment that the curators express repeatedly in *The International Style* and other publications both before and after Exhibition 15: American engineers had quite capably produced the

Lockwood & Greene, Necco Factory, Cambridgeport, Massachusetts. View of chimney and process pipes

"new architecture" outside of any aesthetic considerations. Taken from Le Corbusier's famous dictum to heed the advice of American engineers but ignore American architects, this attitude was given lively expression in Barr's course on modern art at Wellesley, which required a visit to the Necco factory in Cambridgeport, Mass.[24]

Despite many similarities in conception, there was a moment when the book and exhibition proposal necessarily diverged, if only due to the exigencies of their respective formats. In considering how the International Style message might be presented in exhibition form it is interesting to speculate as to whether the *Weissenhofsiedlung*, which Barr, Hitchcock and Johnson had visited, played a role in the formulation of the December proposal.[25] The Stuttgart exhibition's tripartite program of actual buildings, industrial exhibits and a drawings and models exhibition (which consisted primarily of unbuilt work) is discernible in the proposal for an exhibition of models, industrial exhibits and international competition projects.

Perhaps the greatest divergence between the book and the December exhibition proposal is their relative emphases on "the style." In late August Johnson had characterized the book as "about the style and nothing but the style"; the proposal, on the other hand, makes no mention of "style" or the phrase *international style* even though the latter had achieved a certain currency with the curators by then. In a letter to Mumford written just after the December proposal was submitted Johnson argues, "[Wright] is better than Perret or Berlage, more advanced if you will but he has nothing to say today to the International Group."[26] Mumford, who was Wright's champion and whose writings are pointedly based on a nonstylistic rationale, obviously would not have agreed. In fact, his considerable correspondence with Hitchcock prior to the International Style project frequently focused on their ongoing debate on

Wright's significance. Nevertheless, Mumford and his circle (despite their reservations about Hitchcock, Barr and Johnson and their fears of the "superficiality of the eventual staging") could see the proposal as "good—really very good considering."[27]

The evenhandedness of the first proposal (which would ebb and flow during the exhibition's development) certainly reflects a recognition on the curators' part of the political climate in American architectural circles. A letter from Mies to Le Corbusier illuminates the situation: "Especially in Germany, the land of organizers, it seems necessary to emphasize with clarity that architecture is something other than raw functionalism. In Germany the fight against the rationalists will be harder than against the academicians."[28] If Mies in 1929 could characterize the battles with the academy as being to some extent a thing of the past, the same could not be said of the contemporaneous situation in America. Hitchcock frequently assured Mumford that their differences in opinion were not substantial within a broader debate.[29] Similarly, by foregoing their stylistic arguments in the first proposal the curators sought to emphasize the common cause "against the academicians."

Lewis Mumford.

Part Three: Winter 1931

Vladimir Tatlin, Tower of the Third International, 1920. Elevation

The first weeks of the new year were, based on Goodyear's approval, spent organizing the exhibition committee and preparing a revised proposal for the trustees' formal approval. On January 8 Goodyear, Barr, Johnson *père,* Johnson *fils* and Blackburn held a meeting where it was confirmed that museum trustee Stephen Clark would chair the exhibition committee and that Johnson, until then the proposed committee secretary, would be the exhibition director. Nine days later Clark chaired another meeting of the committee, where it was decided to revise and expand the December memo and tentative budget for resubmission to the trustees.[1] It was also decided to print a pamphlet to describe the exhibition "for private circulation." The responsibility for the revisions and the pamphlet both fell to Johnson.

The February proposal (see appendix 2) has several important innovations, mostly elaborations of ideas expressed in the first proposal. However, there is one major change: the elimination of the international competition. The reasons were not financial, as the prize money in the first budget is simply reallocated in the revised budget. Although it is possible that Goodyear or the trustees objected to the idea of a competition at the museum, in subsequent years a number of such events were part of the museum's programs.[2] More likely, the decision was logistic, caused by either lack of time or exhibition space.

In any event, as the competition is eliminated, the first section is expanded. While it still refers to an exhibition of "models by American and foreign architects," the revised proposal suggests that the models be accompanied by "explanatory plans, elevations and perspectives" and that "actual buildings by these architects will also be shown."

The mention of photographs representing "actual" buildings strongly suggests that the curators intended that the models represent projected works. While the decision to showcase unbuilt works might seem contrary to the curators' expressed preferences, it is made clear that if the projected works could be built or, preferably, be works in progress, they would more closely suit the curators' purposes. Furthermore, the decision to add photographs of actual buildings might have served to legitimize the projected works. Barr's dismissive attitude toward the Russian Constructivists and El Lissitzky mirrors the curators' anxieties about architectural projects. His references to the work of the former as "romantically impossible *projets*" and the latter as "prophetic fiction" are a sweeping rejection of utopian and theoretical work, regardless of aesthetic orientation.[3] In addition to a connoisseurial predisposition, the curators were also considering the exhibition's reception: "Things actually constructed have much more propaganda force in America than any project could possibly have."[4]

The inclusion of photographs and expansion of the specified explanatory material are also reminiscent of Barr's suggestion that Hitchcock expand the illustrative material in *Modern Architecture*. The type of explanatory material is interesting. In many discussions of the importance of plans the curators' rhetoric is a near paraphrase of Le Corbusier's aphorism "the plan is the generator."[5] In their aesthetic arguments, however, the curators back away from absolute endorsement of the plan alone:

> The essence of architecture lies in the relation of the various sorts of geometrical projections. The realities of function must appear in the elevations. Even the functionalists who deny the necessity for aesthetic expression must admit that the essential character of the plan is generally apprehended from the exterior of the building. The contemporary exaggeration of the plan is primarily an architect's game.[6]

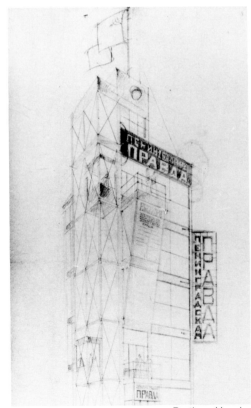

Brothers Vesnin,
Pravda Building, 1923.

Richard Neutra, 1930.

Richard Neutra, bus design, 1931. Perspective

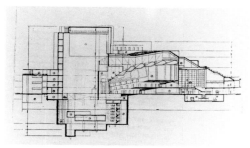

Norman Bel Geddes, Kharkov Theater Competition, 1930. Section

There is no mention of the section, which, of any drawing type, is certainly the "architect's game." For an exhibition that was to have a general as well as a professional audience, sections might not have been entirely appropriate. However, there are no sections in *Modern Architecture* and only one in *The International Style*, both of which had a considerably more astute readership. Despite the curators' emphasis on image and appearance, they did not recognize that two of the International Style's principles, volumetric assembly and asymmetrical composition, were often most forcefully expressed in section.

The list of proposed architects remains the same but for the addition of Richard Neutra who brought the number to six Americans and four Europeans. Neutra's original exclusion and subsequent inclusion are curious. Hitchcock had written very positively about Neutra's work, saying that he was the "most important" architect of the new style in the United States,[7] and his work is cited in the proposal as evidence of modern activity in America. Furthermore, Johnson's father secured for Neutra the commission to design an all-aluminum bus for mass production.[8]

Aside from the more substantive changes, many elements of the December proposal are given more definition in the revised version. The first proposal's tentative pairing of architects with building types is completed, creating a broad list of different construction and use types that demonstrate the "extent of achievement" in modern design. In most cases the pairings can be ascribed to particular projects admired by the curators: Bel Geddes presenting a theater (the Kharkov Theater Competition); Hood, a skyscraper (the McGraw-Hill Building); Howe & Lescaze, a school (Oak Lane Country Day School); Wright, a country home (various projects); Gropius, an apartment house (various projects); and Oud, a public building (Kiefhoek church). The associations of the Bowman Brothers with a prison and Le Corbusier with a department store

Richard Neutra, "Rush City Reformed," 1928-31
(With Ain, Dovell and Wordlar). Aerial perspective

Frank Lloyd Wright, Taliesin III, Wisconsin, 1925.

are less clear or perhaps, in the latter case, a mistake on the curator's part. Despite remarkable knowledge of contemporary events Barr, Hitchcock, and Johnson were not omniscient; for example, they believed that Guevrekian had designed the Comte de Noailles's villa and refer to *Casabella* magazine as "Plaza Bella." Neutra's linkage with a "community housing project" was certainly based on his previously published Rush City Revisited proposals, the only direct reference to an ideal projection.

The section previously referred to as "industrial exhibits" is renamed "Solutions to Three American Building Problems." The titles of the three exhibits, "City Building," "Factory Organization" and "Housing Project for Minimum Wage Earners," are slight expansions on the previous proposal. However, it is in the descriptions of the exhibits that the most elaboration occurs.

Walter Gropius, Siemensstadt
Housing Development, Berlin, 1930.
Corner buildings with balconies

In a brief statement on the "problems of urban building" Johnson defines "modern" city planning as the extension of the "well-planned house or office building"—a reductive technocratic analogy with anti-skyscraper undertones that one might associate with the *sachlich* movement rather than with the International Style. However, Johnson's functionalist critique of the skyscraper is anticipated in Barr's and Hitchcock's previously published attacks on that particular construction type. These are mainly formal arguments, whereas Johnson's functionalist critique is a new tack in the "battle against the skyscraper."[9] Even so, the curators' position on skyscrapers in the proposal is, ultimately, conflicted: even as Johnson characterizes their existence as a result of poor planning, the curators hope that the "style" might redeem them as aesthetic monuments. Demonstrating this ambivalence is the inclusion of both Neutra with his Rush City proposal (which was, in part, a critique of high-rise urban construction) and Hood with a proposed skyscraper design.

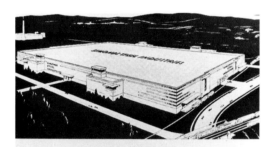

Windowless Building now under construction for the Simonds Saw and Steel Company, Fitchburg, Mass. The Austin Company, Engineers and Builders. An attempt to attain lighting by artificial methods with intensities that do not vary. Mechanical ventilation is provided. It remains to be proved that the artificial atmosphere and lighting are equal in all respects to natural methods.

The Austin Company, Engineers & Builders, Simonds Saw and Steel Factory, Fitchburg, Massachusetts, 1930. Aerial perspective

The curators' negative attitudes toward high rises would have found support in the writings of reformist urban critic Lewis Mumford. The curators, who all spoke highly of Mumford, were familiar with his arguments against the skyscraper which turn frequently on issues of density and light. It is thus doubly ironic that Starrett Brothers is again proposed as "curator" of the construction section. As the builder was following up the Empire State Building with the Starrett-Lehigh loft building (two of Manhattan's densest urban developments), Starrett would probably not have been sympathetic to Mumford's or the curators' concerns.

While Johnson and Mumford share a bit of common ground on the issue of skyscrapers, their respective analyses and solutions to the problem are radically different. Mumford's socio-functional position regards the "subordination of human values and needs to possibilities of commercial profiteering" as a deterrent to the creation of livable cities.[10] Johnson is more inclined to accommodate established financial interests, and his presentation of the ideal factory and minimum-wage workers' housing is geared to the viewpoint of industrial capital. The problem of the workplace and housing was well established in the early twentieth century by the writings of such reformers as Jacob Riis and by such calamities as the 1911 Triangle Shirt Waist Company fire. Sidestepping the liberal to progressive (not to mention syndicalist and socialist) positions associated with the reform and revolutionary movements, Johnson describes the ideal workplace as a "windowless factory artificially lighted and ventilated." (The Austin Company, Engineers and Builders, actually built such a factory for the Simonds Saw and Steel Company in Fitchburg, Mass., published in the February 1931 issue of *Architectural Record*.) As horrific as this sounds today, Johnson does obliquely refer to the reformist demands for adequate light and air in the workplace but subsumes them behind a façade of technical prowess.

Johnson's framing of the housing "problem" is a similar appeal to industry. Without referring to any particular need for housing, or the cause of it, Johnson notes that private industry achieves a return of "but 25% on capital invested in low cost housing."[11] The exhibit is to demonstrate methods of lowering construction costs (thereby increasing profits) without lowering "standards of living conditions." Johnson's interest in the Bowman Brothers, whom he describes as "primarily steel engineers,"[12] also appears to be technocratic. The project that first attracted his notice was an all-metal prefabricated house design, which he took to various builders and industrialists for their opinions on its feasibility.

Granted, Johnson's interests in this regard are framed to support "the style." Nevertheless, it is Johnson who first undertakes to rationalize the authors' arguments with references to the financial framework and the purely technical aspects of construction. Just after the proposal was accepted by Goodyear Johnson writes to Mumford: "I am planning to have models by the great architects, but I want somehow, too, to emphasize the importance of planning in any architecture of the present. In other words, not too much aesthetics."[13] In this regard the proposed exhibition began to assume a broader scope than the book and, in many instances, the book became more a point of departure than a point of reference. It is useful, therefore, to reconsider the roles of Hitchcock, Johnson and Barr in relation to the development of the exhibition. While Johnson clearly played the junior role to Hitchcock in developing the book, exhibition documents reveal a surprising level of leadership on Johnson's part. Hitchcock's name is not mentioned in the proposal, he is not designated a member of the official committee and is not mentioned in the minutes of the committee's meetings as having been present. In the budget, funds are provided for Johnson's and Blackburn's expenses and Mies's honorarium, but again no mention is made of Hitchcock.

One cannot infer that Johnson somehow threw over Hitchcock or that the exhibition evolved without Hitchcock's formidable intellectual influence. Nevertheless, in the first proposals Johnson is defining his role in the project along with the curators' shared and overriding concern with "the style." The extent to which Barr allowed him to do so, in addition to appointing him exhibition director, underscores the confidence that Barr placed in Johnson's capabilities, remarkable considering that the latter had little other than his travels to recommend him as the director of the museum's first architecture exhibition.

Barr's faith in the unproven young critic was not wholly unprecedented in the museum's brief history. In selecting Barr as the museum's first director, the trustees showed willingness to take certain risks in charting the course of the new institution. Of his appointment, Barr writes: "The fact that you are even considering me as a possible participant in this great scheme has set my mind teeming with ideas and plans. This is something I could give my life to—unstintedly."[14] In turn, Barr extended the confidence placed in him to others and frequently relied on criteria other than standard credentials in selecting his lieutenants in the "great scheme." Like Barr, Hitchcock had no doctoral degree, and curator and later director of the Department of Architecture and Design (1951–1987) Arthur Drexler was appointed without an undergraduate degree. Johnson had certain qualities, in addition to his instinctive critical sense, that contributed to Barr's estimation of his capabilities: his wealth and his willingness.

Johnson's commitment of his personal wealth and efforts is important not for his historical aggrandizement but for the direct way in which they affected the exhibition.[15] As the exhibition proposal was revised and expanded, Johnson took increasing responsibility for its appearance and content.

Clauss & Daub, House for Pinehurst, N.C., 1931. Model

Johnson alone had the means to be a true connoisseur. The element of patronage intertwined in the exhibition program was certainly not foreign to him. Despite Johnson's growing attraction to and identification with architects, his language continues to reflect a residual attitude of upper-class patronage, particularly with regard to the commissioning of interiors. In describing Abby Rockefeller's decision to commission Donald Deskey to design her private art gallery Johnson writes that the "client ordered his apartment through an American,"[16] the syntax emphasizing the prerequisites of the patron. In his later correspondence with Mies Johnson is respectful if not obsequious. However, in trying to convince his mother that Mies should redesign his apartment Johnson writes, "There is this very great architect here that does the best interiors in the world."[17] As a further inducement Johnson informed his mother that a Mies-designed apartment would be "the first room in *my* latest style in America."[18] While the language reflects Johnson's cajoling of his mother, the possessive pronoun is consistent with the acquisitorial privilege of patronage. Oud most keenly felt Johnson's dual roles of champion *and* patron of architects. In the summer of 1930 Johnson suggested that his family hire Oud to design a house for their property at Pinehurst, North Carolina, and in June 1931 Oud agreed to accept the commission.[19] While Johnson was quite supportive of the final project, he was also obliged to convey to Oud his mother's reactions and other comments that focused principally on the orientation of the guest bedrooms and bathrooms.[20] Clauss & Daub were also asked to submit designs for the Pinehurst project.[21] Although neither of the Pinehurst proposals was executed, Oud's project and Johnson's Mies-designed apartment were featured in the exhibition. Johnson's connoisseurial patronage extended beyond architectural commissions. In addition to studying contemporary building, a certain amount of Johnson's 1930 trip to Europe was devoted to negotiating purchases of drawings by Le Corbusier,[22] a painting by Mondrian and German furniture and lighting fixtures for himself, his mother and Alfred and Marga Barr.

Donald Deskey, Print Room Gallery, Rockefeller Apartment, NYC, 1931.

Along with Johnson's ability to indulge his connoisseur's inclinations were other privileges of wealth, most notably access to other people in places of power to support the curators' propaganda efforts. In letters written in the summer of 1930 Johnson displays a growing awareness of the importance of this access: "I must see the construction men and see where they got it and how much they are really worth [while] and helpful to me. . . . Especially must I start to find the ways and means of the economic side. There is no reason why in the next few years I should not combine study, pure study, with working into the practical side, of working with people, getting to know them, and *soignant mes relations*."[23]

The extension of the exhibition's scope to include and define a role for industrial capital is certain evidence of Johnson's quick learning. His "working into the practical side" is most often cited by critics as the undoing of the ideological elements of European modernism at the moment of its introduction to America. In some regards this credits the curators with more than they may have been capable of accomplishing. As Richard Pommer notes, the curators "went further to tame the new architecture than many Europeans," though in many respects their position was strongly supported by contemporary European developments.[24] The alliance between the Deutscher Werkbund and the politically centrist architects in the circle of Mies van der Rohe represented, in some ways, a model for Johnson's appeal to the political and financial status quo. Johnson's description of Mies to Oud is relevant in this regard:

> [Mies] *has closed the Bauhaus for a month because the students were so politically minded after the regime of Hannes Meyer that they thought they would continue to run the school along their programmatic lines. Mies says he has no interest whatsoever in politics or programs but only in beautiful buildings, so he has closed the school. I have great hopes for the Bauhaus if Mies can once* [sic] *get his start there.*[25]

It is interesting to compare Johnson's stance with other contemporary American positions. Buckminster Fuller's 4D House proposal of 1929 sought a completely different solution to the problem of "unintelligent building." Railing against aestheticism, which he claims can "find beauty even in a lie,"[26] Fuller proposes an intimate partnership with industrial capital to mass produce prefabricated houses. Severely proscribing the role of architects (and International Style propagandists), Fuller declares, "Stylistic differences in the creation of the new industrially-to-be-produced [sic] house would spell its defeat. It must be functionally designed, dynamically balanced and harmoniously presented."[27] Johnson and Fuller, both sons of the upper class and Harvard graduates, could not have been further apart in attitude though they shared common operational methods. Both attempted directly to enlist the powerbrokers of the day: *Built To Live In* (a prospectus for Exhibition 15 by Johnson) and Fuller's *4D Time Lock* were both circulated "privately" to government leaders and captains of industry. Both authors made conspiratorial though transparently insincere requests that the material be kept "confidential."

At first glance, Johnson's proposal that the Bowman Brothers design a prison appears somewhat odd. Johnson's letters, however, further reveal his nascent ability to recognize opportunities created by his access to powerbrokers: in explaining his suggestion to the architects Johnson points out that the secretary of the museum's Board of Trustees, Samuel Lewisohn, was also on the New York State commission on prisons and, hence, a possible source of commissions.[28] While nothing came of this particular scheme, Johnson's collaborations with his father were more fruitful. Due to the family's connections with the Aluminum Company of America,[29] the Johnsons were in a position to facilitate the design and production of the previously mentioned all-aluminum bus for the White Motor Company in Cleveland. After considering Howe & Lescaze and Mies, Johnson chose Neutra to produce the design.[30] In a similar

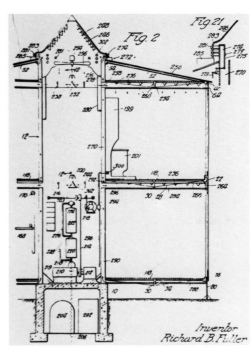

R. Buckminster Fuller, 4D House, 1927. Section

role, the Johnsons obtained a commission for Clauss & Daub to design prototype filling stations for the Standard Oil Company. The buses were not built, but a number of the filling stations were constructed and represented in the exhibition. In an interesting variation on the theme Neutra arranged for Johnson to contact Dutch industrialist C. H. van der Leeuw, and subsequently Johnson introduced van der Leeuw to Abby Rockefeller.[31]

As the exhibition developed, the curators enlisted other ranks of the rich and powerful to support their project in an elaborate campaign of letter writing to those "who have demonstrated a commitment to the movement." Barr and Johnson requested only the use of their names as "patrons" of the exhibition. If the description of a role for private industry served to make "the style" acceptable to financial interests, the enlistment of the Duke of Alva, Viscount Charles de Noailles, Princess Edmond de Polignac and Baroness Helena von Nostitz-Hindenburg, among many lesser titled others, was a powerful appeal to the status-conscious American middle class.

The curators' manipulation of middle-class obsessions with "taste" should not be mistaken as a simple exercise in *épater le bourgeoisie*. Despite their (heretofore) apolitical and elitist stance, Barr and Johnson were not content with an audience of the converted. Many young men of "private means" might have settled into a life of idle elegance. Johnson was certainly not one of them. In a letter to Barr, Johnson responds to a dressing-down from the director: "I did not resent your sermon in the slightest. After all what I want most to do is be influential and if there is a method why not learn it."[32] Sixty years later it is difficult to disassociate this attitude from Johnson's recent "stylistic" approach: a willful exploitation of the formal aspects of high modernism, post-modernism and post-structural philosophical speculation. However, it is clear that in the early 1930s, "the first time [he knew] enough about anything . . . to be boring to people,"[33] Johnson's desire to be influential was synonymous with his desire to promote what he firmly believed to be good architecture. In his letters to Oud, which of all of his correspondence (save that with Barr) are the least guarded, Johnson writes: "I wish I could communicate the feeling of seeing the Bruenn house of Mies. I have only had similar architectural experience before the Hook and in old things [like] the Parthenon."[34]

While many critics' support for the modernist project was based on ideological or political reasons, Johnson was clearly *moved* by modern architecture. From Berlin he relates, "Last night I hardly dreamed of buildings at all. It is a strange fact that not one night has gone by but that I have had some dream on architecture."[35] Johnson's subjective orientation, a sort of architectural rapture, combined with his keen intellect and formidable resources created his new activist mien.

His dedication to the exhibition and the selected architects is striking. Not only did he hire Mies to design his apartment and propose that he design the exhibition, he also sought commissions for the architect with the Rockefellers and the Aluminum Company.[36] He donated his own time to the project for over a year and was largely responsible for its finances.[37] He personally loaned the Bowman Brothers money to complete their model for the exhibition. He convinced his father to donate additional funds and to serve on the exhibition committee. (The elder Johnson's presence on the committee may also have been a display of parental, not to mention lawyerly, concern. Not as convinced, perhaps, as others of his son's capabilities he was horrified to hear that Johnson *fils* was planning to design buildings himself, particularly an addition to the home of a family friend).[38] Through his father Johnson also approached the Aluminum Company for further donations.

Johnson's attempts to be influential on behalf of "the movement" were not limited to financial succor. He lent photographs for the Harvard Society of Contemporary Art's exhibition on the Bauhaus and secured Oud a visiting professorship at Columbia University, which Oud declined.[39] During the exhibition planning, Johnson and Barr involved themselves in a dispute surrounding the annual Architectural League exhibition by organizing a counter-exhibition (the "Rejected Architects" exhibition) of modernist work in a Sixth Avenue storefront.[40] Before Exhibition 15 opened Johnson attempted to organize the "rejected architects" and a number of other young designers in the short-lived American Union for New Architecture.[41] Moreover, Johnson's duties as director of Exhibition 15 were not entirely exalted. With a staff of one the director also found himself packing crates, hanging photographs and rushing off to Buffalo and elsewhere when the exhibit ran into logistical problems. Johnson's earnestness, ambition and money made the exhibition possible without significantly transforming its intellectual spine as crafted principally by Hitchcock.

Pommer contrasts the book's "overtly propagandistic" character with the exhibition's "aura of objectivity."[42] This aura was one of many expediencies opted by the curators. This is evident particularly in the selection of the "nine" architects. While anecdotal histories have it that the inclusion of American architects in Exhibition 15 was a result of a purported clash between the curators and the Board of Trustees, there is no evidence of any such confrontation. In fact, circumstances suggest the opposite. The December proposal, submitted to Goodyear for approval prior to review by the trustees, included more Americans than Europeans. Furthermore, Barr had staged a number of exhibitions exclusively composed of European artists. If the curators can be considered Europhiles, the museum leadership was no less so; all of the trustees who collected paintings owned significant European works. There is little evidence that the museum's independent-thinking patron-supporters would have taken a parochial stand against Barr had he presented a reasoned proposal for an exhibition of European architecture.[43]

When Johnson confides to the Bowman Brothers that the curators "have compromised as little as possible with the modernistic element in American Architecture,"[44] the question is: Compromised with whom? While anecdotes are perhaps more colorful, the selection of architects was certainly the curators' own. It is more useful to consider Johnson's reasonings as expressed at the time of the exhibition:

> Frank Lloyd Wright was included only from courtesy and in recognition of his past contributions; Raymond Hood because some day he may be attracted into the fold by his opportunism; the Bowman Brothers because they are primarily steel engineers and might some day standardize a half-way decent steel house; Neutra and Howe and Lescaze because they are the only successful modern architects in America.[45]

In *The International Style* the authors make no such concessions, and it is here that the clearest distinction can be seen between the book's propagandistic and the exhibition's strategic attitudes. Inasmuch as the exhibition relied on goodwill and support from disparate sources, the curators were mindful of the political implications of their words and deeds and how they might affect the exhibition. While the book had a specific, rather sophisticated readership, the exhibition as envisioned by Johnson was more inclusive—in fact, exhaustively so. To insure the success of the exhibition and, therefore, of "the movement" in America, Johnson attempted to engage (both directly and through the press) not only a broader range of "progressive" architects but builders, financial interests and related professions. Special previews and openings were scheduled for housing advocates, interior decorators, stage designers and the

"Modern Architecture – International Exhibition," Bullocks-Wilshire Department Store,
Los Angeles, 23 July – 30 August 1932. Installation view

directors of university art departments as well as for architects (see part 7).
Perhaps more important than the attempt to engage the various professions was the
extent of the curators' plans to reach the general public, specifically the middle
class. Public lectures were held at the museum and at the various venues around
the country, two of which were department stores (Sears, Roebuck & Co. in Chicago
and Bullock's in Los Angeles[46]). Later in the exhibition planning, Johnson began to
emphasize residential construction, particularly single-family houses, "as the most
interesting exhibit [for the public] is still that of the private house."[47]

Although unstated, there also appears to have been a similarly favorable disposition
toward the program of the school, first expressed in the competition proposal and
later in the association of Howe & Lescaze with a school project. Like the private
house, the school was a widely accessible program type of great interest to the
public.

Every exhibition is to some degree an attempt to convince an audience. What
distinguishes Johnson's efforts was his near messianic zeal. Even as he
collaborated with Hitchcock on *The International Style*, Johnson perceived the need
for three additional publications to accompany the exhibition, despite the financial
pressures imposed by the Depression.[48] Between the time of Exhibition 15's
conception and its opening Johnson proposed two other shows, one of which (the
"Rejected Architects" exhibition) was staged. Similarly, he drew up a list of potential
European and Japanese venues and contacts even as the curators were
overwhelmed with the task of setting up a difficult American itinerary.
Much has been written about the project's "international character;"[49] in
Johnson's mind, it was "global":

> *From Vienna, from Helsingfors and from Tokyo reports of modern
> building reach us. Every architectural magazine in the world, and even
> the more popular art digests carry accounts of modern architecture.
> Conservative architects the world over are turning to the modern style.*[50]

Part Four: Spring 1931

Messianic fervor alone was not enough, however, to insure success. In each revised budget estimate the projected costs are reduced (even as Johnson's plans become more grand), reflecting the difficulties of raising funds.[1] After the trustee's approval of the project, which included a financial commitment from the museum, much of the organizational effort was spent on fundraising. Johnson writes, "As with any project of this sort in America today the main question is that of raising money."[2]

Even as costs were being trimmed in the third budget, money was reserved for the printing of Johnson's pamphlet *Built To Live In* [3] (see appendix 3). Printed in March 1931, it was sent to potential supporters, financial and otherwise. Judging by the size of the mailing to museum directors, the curators had narrowed their search for funding to other institutions, solicited as subscribers to the exhibition tour. Of the dozens of institutions approached, by April 1931 the Pennsylvania Museum of Art, the Cleveland Museum of Art and, jointly, the Buffalo Academy of Fine Arts and the Albright Art Gallery[4] had made some form of commitment. In approving the project the trustees had asked that no public announcement be made of the exhibition until some of the money had been raised. In March 1931 with, at best, a third of the funds committed the American architects were officially invited. Even so, the project's tenuous financial condition was obvious, and as the invitations were being extended Goodyear mentioned to the trustees that an alternate exhibition was possible "should the Architecture Exhibition not be held in the Museum's galleries."[5] Like the preliminary proposals, *Built To Live In* makes no mention of the International Style. Johnson commits only that "a group of the most prominent architects of the world will construct models" for the exhibition. To avoid controversy in the fundraising effort Johnson continues to emphasize the broader fight "against the academicians": the work of Hood and Wright, characterized before and after the exhibition as flawed, was said to "bear witness to the widespread nature of the movement."

While no names are proposed for the exhibition in the pamphlet, a certain amount of reading between the lines gives a clue to the identities of the world's "most prominent architects." The text, a slightly expanded version of the February proposal, repeats the latter's account of "modern activity" in America and abroad: Wright, Hood, Neutra, the Bowman Brothers and Le Corbusier are mentioned by name. Furthermore, all "nine" (with the exception of the Bowman Brothers) are represented in the illustrations. The Bowman Brothers had not constructed a single project other than their own offices. Johnson's reluctance to include an illustration of one of their projected works can be explained by the pamphlet's title: the particular emphasis on "built" work indicates the curators' preference for "actual monuments." Bel Geddes is not mentioned, nor is his work illustrated, and his name does not appear again in any documents related to the exhibition.[6]

In addition to being a prospectus of the proposed exhibition, *Built To Live In* served another purpose. Along with a number of articles by Johnson published around this time and the "Rejected Architects" exhibition, it increased the Museum's visibility and introduced Johnson to the architectural community. Hitchcock and Barr had both published various works that identified themselves personally with the "new" architecture. In addition to *Modern Architecture*, Hitchcock's reviews of American and European books and periodicals appeared frequently in *Architectural Record*. Barr's 1928 review of the Necco factory appeared in *The Arts,* as did his survey of the Russian architectural scene the following year. Both Barr and Hitchcock contributed articles in the late 1920s to *The Hound and Horn*. Outside the interlocking circles of the museum and the "Crimson Connection" Johnson was certainly the newcomer, as was the museum itself among the traditional venues of architectural exhibitions. Although anyone who knew Barr would not have been surprised at the proposal (see Notes, page 89) for an architectural exhibition, the museum's

Clauss & Daub, "Lindbergh" House, 1931. Model

first forays into propagandizing modern building must have raised certain expectations as well as trepidations.

If the December proposal's evenhandedness was preserved in *Built to Live In*, the "Rejected Architects" exhibition and Johnson's publications are decidedly partisan. Johnson is considerably more forthcoming about the authors' aesthetic position in his review of Joseph Urban's design for the New School published in March 1931.[7] In that review Johnson bases his critique on the principles of the International Style (volume, irregularity and lack of decoration). He also uses the term "International Style" with uppercase initials.

The "Rejected Architects" exhibition opened in April 1931. Although neither the curators' names nor the name of the museum was mentioned in the pamphlet (see appendix 3) available at the exhibition, the event was widely identified with Barr and Johnson. In the brief text, the pamphlet again referred to the "International Style" and was a précis of the authors' aesthetic position:

Joseph Urban, The New School, NYC, 1931. Principal façade

> *The style is characterized by flexibility, lightness and simplicity. Ornament has no place, since hand-cut ornament is impracticable in the machine age. The beauty of the style rests in the free composition of volumes and surfaces, the adjustment of such elements as doors and windows, and the perfection of machined surfaces.*

Johnson's article on skyscrapers,[8] published a month after the exhibition, makes no reference to the International Style or to the specifically Taylorized arguments of the February proposal but is based on the familiar modernist arguments regarding applied ornament and structural integrity. Johnson's sharp criticisms negatively compare the unadorned Monadnock Building with Cass Gilbert's Woolworth Building, Ralph Walker's Telephone Building and the

Hugh Ferriss, "The Art Center."

Burnham & Root, Monadnock Building, Chicago, 1890-91.

drawings of Hugh Ferriss. The latter, Johnson pointedly notes, "is not an architect," and his drawings are described as "falsely lighted renderings that picture fantastic crags rising high above dark caverns."[9] While the "Rejected Architects" exhibition might have been dismissed by some as a stunt, the architects criticized in print by Johnson were no doubt nonplussed by the twenty-four-year-old critic's sharp remarks. Never one to be accused of "Spenglerian melancholy," Johnson's skyscraper article also departs from standard architectural criticism in that he directs his comments to other critics. Using their own remarks, Johnson rebuts the writings of the supporters of the "skyscraper school": T. E. Tallmadge, the architectural historian; C. H. Edgell, dean of the Harvard School of Architecture; and, incredibly, Fiske Kimball, the director of the Pennsylvania Museum of Art. As Kimball's support for the International Style exhibition was critical to its traveling tour, Johnson's remarks are particularly daring. (Kimball had the last word: a document in the renamed Philadelphia Museum's archives indicates that when Exhibition 15 reached Philadelphia, he added dozens of projects including the Woolworth Building, Hood's Tribune Tower, Joseph Hoffman's Palais Stoclet, Eric Mendelsohn's Einstein Tower and Hans Poelzig's Berlin theater, all of which had been criticized by Barr, Hitchcock and Johnson.[10])

Similarly, Johnson reviews the reviewers in his article on the "Rejected Architects" published in *Creative Art*.[11] Taking Ely Jacques Kahn, Deems Taylor and Douglas Haskell to task, he insists that the "critics of both the Rejected Architects and the League Show have been uncritical."[12] As in the New School critique and the "Rejected Architects" pamphlet Johnson makes multiple references to the International Style.

The curators, once again, planned to spend the summer traveling in Europe. During the last weeks of May Johnson attempted to move ahead with the American architects. Discussions were held with Neutra, the Bowman Bothers, Howe & Lescaze, Hood and Wright to finalize which types of projects they

46

might submit in model form, and a long list of instructions was sent out requesting biographical information and photographic material for the exhibition and catalogue.

From the moment the discussions with the architects began, the proposed survey of building types, as foreseen in the December proposal, seems to have been forgotten. Not only did the architects, understandably, have various proposals of their own, the curators' criteria became more complex. In negotiations with Neutra Johnson decided that he did not want to exhibit models that had been shown before, particularly in the annual Architectural League exhibition or the "Rejected Architects" exhibition. He also came to realize the importance of the single-family house: "I wish to have as many private houses as I can. Indeed I am thinking of suggesting to the architects that they may submit more than one model if one of them is a private house."[13] His concern was no doubt increased by the number of architects who wanted to submit models of multi-family housing, a building type that he had wanted to reserve for Gropius. (None of the European architects, except Mies, were notified until the curators were back in Europe and could make the proposals in person.)

Despite Johnson's attempts to convince Hood to design an urban commercial skyscraper, Hood persisted in proposing to present a model of a "tall apartment tower project for the country" and, unlike the negotiations over the other proposed models, there was no further discussion of Hood's submission.[14] Nevertheless, Johnson continues to refer to the project as a skyscraper throughout the planning phase.

When Howe & Lescaze were invited, Johnson first suggested a school project based on their successful Oak Lane Country Day School, which had been completed in 1929. Recalling the plans for a competition, Johnson further

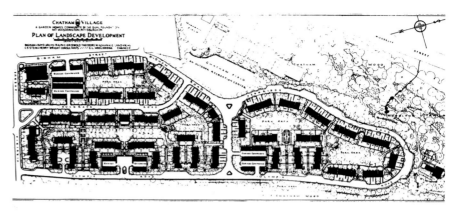

Henry Wright, Chatham Villiage, 1930.

MODEL OF
ALL METAL
APARTMENT
HOUSE
BOWMAN
BROTHERS,
ARCHITECTS

Bowman Brothers, Lake Front Building, 1930.
Model

suggested that it be a prototype design for public schools, and Howe tentatively agreed. Upon seeing the work in progress, Johnson subsequently asked them to submit a model of the Hessian Hills School.

Both the Bowman Brothers and Neutra expressed a desire to present apartment houses. The former, apparently unenthusiastic about the proposal to design a prison, suggested instead "the Apartment House," which may have been the Lake Front Building designed for Chicago and published in the July 1930 issue of *Architectural Record*. Johnson counterproposed that they submit a model of the prefabricated house that they had designed for a minimum-wage earning family— the project that had first caught Johnson's eye. Apparently interested in submitting a large-scale project, they subsequently indicated their willingness to reconsider the prison program. Agreeing on Neutra's project was equally problematic. There were not many viable alternatives to his proposal to design a "series of apartments showing how the bachelor, the married couple and the family should live."[15] He did have a model of the Lovell House but the curators wanted "new" (i.e., previously unpublicized) projects. The curators could have asked Neutra to prepare a completely new, uncommissioned project, but they had no money to cover costs and Neutra had already invested considerable time and expense in his Rush City Revisited proposals. Initial discussions ended with Johnson suggesting the Ring Plan School (a component of Neutra's Rush City project). Johnson's preference for the Ring Plan School over the Lovell House is further evidence of the curators' secondary programmatic interest: educational buildings.

The curators encouraged Wright to submit a model of a private "country house," which appears to have been acceptable to the architect, although at various points during the exhibition planning Wright considered sending more than one model.

Richard Neutra, Lovell House, Los Angeles, 1927. Model

The industrial section also began to take form. No mention is ever made of Starrett Brothers agreeing to participate nor is the "urban construction" exhibit mentioned again, although one photograph of the Starrett-Lehigh building was later included in the exhibition. Throughout the summer Johnson continued to express confidence that the Austin Company would present not one but two models. In an interesting addition to the industrial program, Johnson also invited van der Leeuw to submit a model of the van Nelle factory, designed by van der Lugt & Brinckman. Before leaving for Europe Johnson also appears to have agreed to a model of Henry Wright's Chatham Village project as the centerpiece of the housing exhibit.

In addition to discussions regarding the models, the curators requested that the architects send photographs of "all projects and executed works." Understandably, this blanket directive caused slight consternation among the architects. Regardless of the curators' belief to the contrary, the Bowman Brothers had no executed works; Howe & Lescaze had a number of projects that they were not interested in having exhibited or published (they responded by requesting to design their exhibit themselves); and Neutra preferred to display the entire Rush City proposal. The directive also, in the case of Wright, was the first of many misunderstandings that would turn acrimonious. Wright, who had been in practice for over four decades, received the same instructions as the younger exhibitors. The curators never intended to display more than five or six photographs of each architect's work. Unaware of these guidelines, Wright sent two crates of drawings and photographs to New York at his own expense.

Part Five: Summer 1931

Thus when Johnson sailed for Europe on May 29, a large part of Exhibition 15 had taken tentative shape. The selection of photographs for exhibition and catalogue was left for the fall. However, a format had been established, as Johnson planned to select the Europeans' photographs and have them enlarged for the exhibition while in Germany. Furthermore, in responding to Howe & Lescaze's request to design their own exhibit, Blackburn indicates that Johnson had already made a preliminary design of the exhibition.[1]

Johnson proceeded directly to Rotterdam to speak with Oud. Whether or not the Johnson family actually intended to execute the project by the Dutch architect is not clear. However, both Barr and Johnson were extremely anxious to have a model of the Pinehurst project in the exhibition. The question was not whether Oud was interested (Johnson had previously suggested the project and Oud replied that he was eager to get "better work in Holland than those damned minimum houses of which I am a 'specialist' now"[2]) but whether the Dutch architect would be able to deliver the model in time for the exhibition. Oud was unmoved by the curators' urgency and told them he would take the commission but was hesitant about working to a schedule. Oud's attitude, which continuously vexed the curators, is frequently expressed in qualifications to his commitment, such as his statement that he will "only send [the model] to the exhibition if it is just as good as I like it."[3] Oud also suggested that he might send a model of the Hook of Holland if he could not complete the new house project. Informed of this back-up plan, Barr suggested instead that they use Oud's Stuttgart *Siedlung*. Hitchcock suggested his church at Kiefhoek but Barr felt it "would provoke a great deal of irrelevant antagonism."[4]

From the Netherlands Johnson traveled on to Germany and met with Gropius. Despite earlier predictions there is no documentation to suggest that the architect was interested in designing an apartment house, and it was decided that Gropius would submit a model of the Bauhaus school.

Le Corbusier, Swiss Dormitory, Cité Universitaire, Paris, 1932. Model

While Johnson was in Rotterdam, Barr and Hitchcock were in Paris. Barr was working principally on the upcoming Matisse exhibition and contacting potential patrons for Exhibition 15. It fell to Hitchcock to discuss the exhibition with Le Corbusier. While it isn't clear exactly which project the curators had in mind when they suggested that Le Corbusier might submit a "department store," soon after their arrival in France a model of the Villa Savoye was commissioned. Discussions continued as to whether or not a model of the Swiss Pavilion at the Cité Universitaire (like the Bauhaus, programmatically related to education) should also be included, although the additional costs appear to have caused the curators to hesitate.[5]

Even though the curators apparently had decided on a model of the Tugendhat House in advance of the trip, Johnson and/or Mies seem to have had second thoughts. One letter from Johnson to Barr suggests allowing Mies to design a new house project or, alternatively, to submit the existing model of the Stuttgart "department store," the Brenninckmeyer project based on the Stuttgart Bank Building project of 1928.[6]

Johnson met with Haesler and on the spot agreed to accept the previously exhibited model of the Rothenberg housing development for the Industrial section.[7] Whether this was to be exhibited with or to replace Henry Wright's project is unclear, but the Chatham Village model is not mentioned again with regard to the Housing section. Correspondence also indicates that further attempts to obtain a model of the van Nelle factory were unsuccessful. Van der Leeuw declined to lend the model and even his name as a patron if "people like Hood would exhibit; only if there were *really* modern European and American architects."[8]

Mies van der Rohe, Brenninckmeyer Department Store, 1929.

If the curators' discussions with the American architects produced some unanticipated results, by the time the curators returned to Europe they had revised their original conception of the role of models in the exhibition rather subtly. All of the European projects considered, with the exception of Oud's house for Pinehurst and Mies's "department store," were already constructed or in construction. The decision to include built works by the Europeans and unbuilt works by Americans is partially explained in a statement by Barr about the European models made in response to Johnson's suggestion that Mies design a new house:

> About models. I still feel it better from the public's point of view to have models of things already built. Why have Mies design a new house which would be of interest only in Europe now that the show would probably not come to Europe? Why not have him do the Brno house since it is the largest and most luxurious private house in the style?[9]

The statement is oblique at best, but Barr appears to suggest that models of projected works are only of interest as novelties and even then only locally. As such the European projects were seen in a different light: while the American projects were news and heralded the arrival of the International Style in the United States, the European projects were recast as evidence of the legitimacy of the new architecture. In this regard, the Tugendhat House, "the largest and most luxurious private house in the style," assumed special importance.

Mies's rise in the curators' estimation following Johnson's visit to Brno in the summer of 1930 is one of the truly new, and perhaps the most important, developments in the International Style project over Hitchcock's *Modern Architecture*. The curators saw more than luxury and found the design intellectually challenging. Johnson compares it favorably with Oud's Hook of

Holland, which as a city housing project was certainly not luxurious. Johnson further describes it as an "example of the interdependence of technics and aesthetics in architecture,"[10] and of all the projects in the exhibition catalogue the Tugendhat House is most thoroughly described in spatial terms.

Nonetheless, the house's luxuriousness was never far from the curators' minds. In a letter to Oud Johnson states:

> It has cost so far nearly a million marks so it ought to be good. The main room which serves as dining room, living room, and library is twenty-seven meters long and the wall is entirely of glass as is one of the side walls at least ten meters long. The steel posts are clad in chrome, an onyx wall separates the library from the main living room, and a curving wall of some exotic wood makes the dining niche.[11]

Perhaps it is difficult to appreciate, sixty years later, the significance of Mies's exceedingly minimalist use of commodity materials to connoisseurs. The Compte de Noailles' enthusiasm for the exhibition reflects the curators' own predilections:

> I am so struck by your choice of architects and your placing Mies van der Rohe before anybody else. I agree with this and consider that at the actual moment Mies represents by far the most interesting movement not only in his lines, but also in the fact that he at last is brave enough to work in something else than concrete and glass (Namely marble, wood, etc.).[12]

The luxurious quality of Mies's work gave an added edge to the curators' propaganda campaign. Intellectually, it established a benchmark in

Hitchcock's development of a qualitative hierarchy of materials analogous to the rigor of the classical orders: "Brick appears the best material for large and inexpensive construction, tile in the middle range and plate sheathing for exceptional buildings. In the last the architect has the opportunity to seek to the full the possibilities of richness and individual distinction which the contemporary style affords quite as much as the styles of the past."[13] Barr's letter suggests another, more strategic, interest in the material qualities of the Tugendhat House vis-à-vis the exhibition: as the curators began to focus on the private house, the increased emphasis on luxury was not to alienate but entice the middle class.

In addition to dealing with the architects Johnson and Hitchcock spent the summer finishing the book *The International Style*. Johnson continued to solicit photographs while Hitchcock worked on the text. While Johnson's publications of the spring of 1931 hint at the extent of the book's development, Hitchcock's letters of the following months confirm it. In early June he sent Mumford a draft of the last chapter (on housing) for his comments.[14] By early August Hitchcock was in Berlin to see the Bauaustellung, and Johnson writes: "Russell and I have figured out that we have enough pictures for the book. I am to have another chance at criticizing it and hope to be able to make some helpful changes."[15] By the end of October the final text was complete, two-and-a-half months before the catalogue.[16]

While in Berlin Johnson also continued to search for a German publisher for the book and seems to have reached some sort of agreement with Hoffman Verlag of Stuttgart to publish a German edition. The complexities of Hitchcock's arguments in the volume are due, no doubt, to the continued hope for a dual publication. Recognizing the vastly different situations in America and Europe, the authors support their aesthetic propositions with two interwoven arguments that attempt to address, alternately, American and Continental issues. A good portion of the book, particularly the chapter on functionalism, concerns a principally European debate.[17] The authors' position squarely supports the ideology of those architects (particularly Mies) associated with *Der Ring*. Their position was essentially apolitical and, in opposition to the tenets of *Die Neue Sachlichkeit*, proscribed functionalism as a generator of form. The significance of this debate could only be understood in light of the two preceding decades of architectural development. In a European publication the authors' position would have been accessible, even in the "popular" format suggested by Barr. To accommodate an American readership the authors were in the awkward position of having to explain the *sachlich* argument even as they disputed it. Even to an architecturally literate American reader, the European debate (as simplified by the authors) might have seemed, at best, to have been a tempest in a tea pot. Despite the apparently irreconcilable differences between the two positions, the authors note that "the works of the European functionalists usually fall within the limits of the international style" and that "they may be claimed as its representatives."[18]

Interwoven with the European argument is a critique of the American architectural establishment. As opposed to the complexity of the former, the latter is a basic lesson in the ABC's of the International Style. This involves discrediting not only the academy but the architecture that had to that point been considered "modern." As opposed to the European "functionalists," who had the wrong ideology but produced the right style, the "modernistic" American architects had the right ideology (i.e., apolitical) but produced the wrong style.

Mention has been made of the financial difficulties of the curatorial process. By the summer of 1931 Johnson felt some of these personally, as a run on the

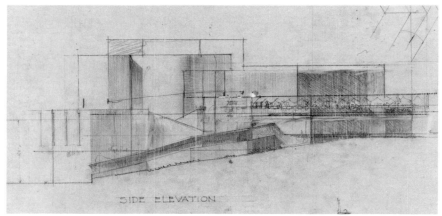

SIDE ELEVATION

Frank Lloyd Wright, New Theater, 1931.

German banks caused him to lose most of the money he had brought to Europe for the summer's expenses. Yet no documents indicate that the curators ever questioned the need for two publications, and additional money was budgeted to pay Hitchcock for his contributions to the catalogue.

The need for an official catalogue, though conceived as propagandistic rather than documentary, apparently overrode any consideration of cost. While the catalogue was complementary to the exhibition, it was certainly redundant conceptually vis-à-vis the book. The importance of the latter is easier to comprehend: the book was certain to achieve wider and longer circulation than the exhibition or the catalogue. The book was also capable of communicating the more subtle points of the curators' arguments. The economic situation in Europe did have some effect on the curators' plans: the exhibition's international tour was seen as less and less likely, and Johnson declined to act on the list of potential exhibitors drawn up the previous spring.

On August 15 Johnson cabled Blackburn:

FOUR OR FIVE MODELS STARTED ENLARGEMENTS ALMOST DONE NEW YORK ABOUT TENTH FEEL WORK IS ALMOST DONE[19]

Before sailing Johnson returned to Brno to see the Tugendhat House once more. Writing to Oud he describes the "prophetic nature of Mies's own character." Johnson closes with this observation of the curatorial process: "I shall never try to do such another show. There are so many disappointments and difficulties and then, too, it is too much work. I want to learn something more some day."[20]

Part Six: Autumn 1931

Frank Lloyd Wright, Standarized Gas Station, 1932.

Barr, Hitchcock and Johnson returned to New York in the fall. Barr was readying the Matisse and Rivera exhibitions that were to precede Exhibition 15, while Hitchcock was teaching at Wesleyan, finishing the manuscript of *The International Style* and preparing his contributions to the catalogue. Johnson joined Blackburn in continuing the exhibition planning.

Some of the arrangements made with the American architects had begun to unravel over the summer. Johnson's request for photographs of all of the architects' built works put the Bowman Brothers in the unenviable position of having to inform the curators that they had not, in fact, built anything other than their own office interiors. When Blackburn notified Johnson in Berlin, he cabled back: "BE SURE THEY ARE ACTUALLY BUILDING SOMETHING OTHERWISE SORRY WE MUST LEAVE THEM OUT."[1] Upon returning, Johnson wrote to them: "Since I hardly dare to make an exhibition of an architectural firm which has built nothing, you will understand that in that case there are many deserving young architects whom I should have to take into the exhibition."[2] Two weeks later Johnson went to Chicago to see the Bowman Brothers. The Chicago architects were apparently successful in eliciting some sympathy from Johnson. After his return to New York he wrote to them confirming their participation and agreeing to exhibit a model of the Lux Apartments, a commissioned project and that appeared to have a chance of being built. The prison project is not mentioned again thereafter.

In Taliesin Wright continued working on the House on the Mesa and notified the curators that he was constructing a second model of a theater, most probably the New Theater project designed in 1931 for Woodstock, N.Y.[3] Wright was also working on a third model of a gas station, most likely the Standarized Gas Station project of 1932, which he sent to New York with the House on the Mesa.[4]

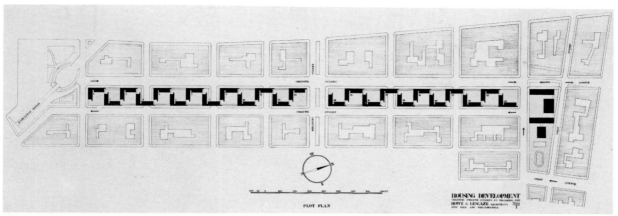

Howe & Lescaze, Chrystie-Forsyth Housing, 1931.

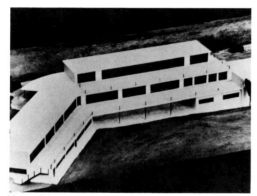

Howe & Lescaze, Hessian Hills School, Croton-on-Hudson, NY, 1931. Preliminary model

Over the summer Blackburn forwarded Howe & Lescaze's proposal to present a model of a housing development (the Chrystie-Forsyth Housing project) rather than a model of the Hessian Hills School project. The exchange further clarifies the curators' attitude toward the models: "GLAD TO GIVE HESSIAN MODEL IF YOU INSIST BUT SCHOOL WILL BE ACTUALLY CONSTRUCTED AT TIME OF SHOW AND NOT SAME AS MODEL."[5] Johnson originally tried to convince them to submit the Hessian Hills model by suggesting he would also consider letting them exhibit the Philadelphia Saving Fund Society (PSFS) tower but eventually relented: "LESCAZE HOUSING ALL RIGHT IF CHANCE OF BEING BUILT ALFRED FAVORS BUILT THINGS."[6]

Most likely, Johnson's decision to leave the Bowman Brothers in the exhibition was due in part to inertia. Nevertheless, a memorandum sent to the subscribing museums in September 1931 (prior to the meeting with the Bowman Brothers) indicates an ongoing ambivalence regarding the models selected. Apparently, with fewer than five months until the opening, Johnson was considering a number of alternate models for the traveling portion of the exhibition. In the memo (see appendix 4) Johnson indicates that Neutra and Gropius would submit models of houses (no doubt the Lovell House and the Bauhaus Director's House, respectively) and that Le Corbusier and the Bowman Brothers would be submitting models of the Swiss Pavilion and a prison project, respectively. These representations are, of course, contrary to all discussions to date and represent an entirely new effort to expand the material in the exhibition.

Johnson's late initiative is not further documented but its chances of succeeding were wholly dependent on more funding for the additional models. As with a number of his attempts to expand the scope of the project, this initiative was frustrated by the realities of the Depression. The memo was

58

circulated to the sixteen institutions committed, in some form, to hosting the exhibition. Of those, almost half withdrew their commitment (see appendix 5).

Aside from Johnson's subsequent trip to Chicago to confront the Bowman Brothers the subscriber's memorandum was Johnson's last effort to alter the proposed roster of principal architects and models. Despite the original conception of the models as representing a survey of modern building types, this final consideration further emphasizes the curators' preference for private houses and schools. At some point during the nearly year-long process, all of the proposed architects (save Hood) were associated with one or both of these building types.

While time and money may have discouraged Johnson from further altering the principal section of the exhibition, he continued to develop other elements of the project. With only three-and-a-half months left in the planning process, he approached the participating architects to write essays to be included in the catalogue. Howe & Lescaze were asked to write something "on the difficulties that a modern architect has with clients and contractors"[7] and the Bowman Brothers were asked to submit an essay on the "Myth of Building Laws," an account of the bureaucratic difficulties that "confront the architect who wishes to build in the modern style."[8]

No account remains of Johnson asking Hood, Wright, or Neutra for similar material, although Wright's essay "Of Thee I Sing," published under very different circumstances after the exhibition's opening, may have been originally solicited as one of the catalogue essays.

At some point during the fall, the Industrial section became known simply as the "Housing section" with no further attempts to stage exhibits of urban construction or windowless factories. Johnson's vision of "an integrated and

decidedly rational mode of building"[9] was influenced, no doubt, by
Le Corbusier's proposals for the "great collaboration of modern times": the
connection des élites that would contribute to the realization of the new age's
great projects. Johnson's inability to muster the support of even a few local
captains of industry was undoubtedly a sobering experience.

Mumford has been historically associated with the Housing section: Clarence
Stein, Henry Wright and Catherine Bauer are also acknowledged in the
catalogue for "assisting in preparing the housing section of the Exhibition."[10]
Apparently, however, Mumford's personal involvement was minimal. The roles
of Stein, Wright and Bauer are unclear. Robert Wojtowicz's ongoing research
on Mumford indicates that throughout most of the planning of Exhibition 15
Mumford was working on the manuscript of The Brown Decades. In a letter to
Wright he describes his role in the project: "I have written the introduction to the
Housing Section of the show: but have scrupulously kept out of suggesting
items even for that tiny piece of it: the whole thing represents Hitchcock and
Johnson."[11] Mumford's disowning of the Housing section may have been
exaggerated slightly to mollify Wright's anger at the way he was portrayed in the
exhibition. (see part 7. Mumford had acted as an intermediary for the museum
in inviting the architect and no doubt was concerned that Wright may have felt
betrayed.) A more comprehensive depiction of the development of the Housing
section can be traced: beyond the essay Mumford was probably only
peripherally involved. Stein, Henry Wright and Bauer, fellow members of the
Regional Planning Association of America,[12] were perhaps more active in
consulting and providing photographs of American projects. Bauer was
principally responsible for the exhibition text panels.[13] Mumford, despite his
denials, probably had some role through the RPAA members in editing or
consulting on both photographs and the texts.[14] The photographs of the
European projects were selected, with or without consultation, from those that
Hitchcock and Johnson had collected for their book. While Johnson may have

consulted with the RPAA members to some extent, his unilateral decision to present the Haesler model (rather than the Henry Wright project) indicates the organization of the Housing section was, like the rest of the exhibition, principally Johnson's responsibility.

Ultimately the continued participation of Mumford and the other RPAA members hinged on various points of agreement among many disagreements. The historical position of Wright's work and the notion of style itself remained points of contention. The architects proposed for the exhibition, particularly Hood, caused further disagreements. Yet Mumford is capable of describing the project as a worthy effort even if "a mixed one, with both good and bad stuff in it [which] seems to me almost inevitable."[15] Despite his objections and his subsequent falling-out with the curators (Hitchcock's and Mumford's long-running correspondence ceased for a number of years after Exhibition 15 opened), their mutual points of agreement were significant. Mumford and the RPAA members were as enthusiastic as the curators about Haesler's project and European housing in general.[16] The curators, in the broadest sense, recognized the need for housing and shared Mumford's sense of urgency if not his sociopolitical analysis.[17] Mumford was also somewhat convinced by Hitchcock's arguments regarding Wright's "individualism." Mumford addresses the issue in a letter to Wright:

> I am naturally on your side with respect to everything except "individuality"—which I trust won't make it seem to you that I am not on your side at all. I still cannot conceive of a city in which each separate work of architecture would be conceived in complete freedom.[18]

The issue remained contentious between Mumford and Wright. The writer seeks to clarify his position on the International Style, individualism, and its relationship to capitalism in a long letter written just before Exhibition 15 opened:

> *While the phrase the international style emphasizes all the wrong things architecturally, I think it is a fine sign that men of good will all over the world are beginning to face life in the same way. . . . No one can be merely an American, any more than he can be merely a New Yorker: we shall all be at each other's throats, and have neither civilization or culture left, unless we become increasingly conscious of our common tasks and our common interests: this for architecture as well as anything else. . . . Such individualism as we shall develop must now be expressed through the collective enterprise: there is real scope for it here, and as we humanize industry and reorient our whole culture towards life, the ground for a genuine organic architecture will be prepared . . . true individualism has nothing to fear from that growth. . . . Capitalism could favor an organic architecture only by way of escape: communism will favor it directly by way of growth. These, then, are our differences and agreements.*[19]

Sometime in November 1931, with a few months remaining before the opening, it apparently occurred to Johnson that despite the exhibition title, there was little evidence that "architects the world over are turning to the modern style." As projected, the exhibition of the work of American, Dutch, German and French architects was, ironically, less "global" and more accurately "transnational"—analogous to the title's historical antecedent: the International Style of painting that flourished in Europe in the late Middle Ages. A section was thus added at a very late date, awkwardly titled "The Extent of Modern Architecture." The title reflects its curatorial intent: the international survey of modern architecture was to demonstrate the validity of the "new" style.

For the most part, the thirty-seven architects and forty projects added were known to the curators and were mentioned in their various texts, including *The International Style.* Additional photographs were solicited from various sources. All of the American architects were known to the curators; most were from New York, as were most of the American projects selected. Barr had been to the Soviet Union and may have visited the two Russian projects selected, although they are not mentioned in his "Notes on Russian Architecture." At that late date the exhibited photographs were obtained not from the architects but from the Soviet Photo Agency in New York.[20] Similarly, Hitchcock had visited England on his return voyage at the end of the summer 1930 but it is not certain that he visited the two projects selected, photographs of which were solicited from the architects for the new section. Photographs of the two Japanese projects were furnished by Neutra.[21] The only unsolicited project was Paul Nelson's pharmacy, photographs of which the architect furnished just weeks before the exhibition opened.[22] The balance of the photographs, with the exception of those of Labayen & Aizpurna's Club House and Figini & Pollini's exhibition house, were probably selected from Hitchcock and Johnson's collection of photographic material obtained from various architects during their travels.

The selection of the architects represented in the Extent of Modern Architecture section was, unfortunately, rather haphazard, as the curators were dependent on material at hand or readily available. Moise Ginsberg, Andrei Burov, the brothers Vesnin, Albert Sartoris, Pierre Chareau, Albert Kahn and Giuseppe Terragni all received somewhat positive notices in the curators' writings, in some cases more positive than those of the architects included in the new section.

The curators' selection from the photographs at hand is beyond speculation, both in terms of the principal architects' projects and the new section. Of Neutra's and the Bowman Brothers' work, the curators were pressed to select the five or six appropriate images that available space allowed each architect. In the instance of Le Corbusier and Wright, the task would have been more extensive but little can be ascertained from analyzing that process.

By year's end the curatorial planning was nearly complete, and the last six weeks before the opening, were devoted to producing and installing Exhibition 15.

Part Seven: Winter 1932

The Galleries

Exhibition 15, which opened on 9 February 1932, was the last exhibition in the museum's first galleries, located on the twelfth floor of the Heckscher Building (now known as the Crown Building) at 730 Fifth Avenue.[1] Unfortunately, no architectural plans of the galleries remain in the museum's or in Barr's archives. However, by examining extant installation photos[2] of the various exhibitions held there and newspaper coverage of the museum's opening, the principal spaces can be credibly reconstructed. Although newspaper accounts are oddly conflicting, the report of the *New York Times* seems to be authoritative: The galleries occupy "about 4,430 square feet of office space. About 3,800 square feet is devoted to galleries—one large gallery, three medium-sized galleries and two small galleries. Opening off of the large gallery is a small room which is to be used as a library and reading room."[3]

As no drawings exist, the authorship of the first museum plan is unclear, although one document on the letterhead of Harrie T. Lindeberg details a cost estimate for the proposed work. While Lindeberg was certainly involved, the galleries cannot necessarily be considered solely his work.

In light of Barr's demonstrated architectural tastes, the design of the galleries was curiously "half-modern." The plan consisted of a number of "cabinet"-type rooms, arranged enfilade and defined by thick *poché*. While the budget was not lavish (the total costs were less than twelve thousand dollars), the galleries could have been quite different spatially without increasing costs. A more plausible, though partial, explanation derives from the structural plan of the building,[4] which had been designed for commercial offices. Overlaying the reconstructed plan and the typically eighteen-by-eighteen-foot column grid reveals that the design strategy was to enclose the existing structure to eliminate freestanding columns (which inhibit viewing) and engaged pilasters (which break up the wall surfaces). Inflated for this purpose, the nearly two-foot-

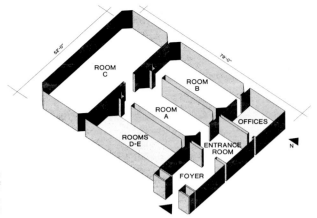

The Museum of Modern Art, N.Y., 730 Fifth Avenue, 1929 – 1932. Axonometric view of reconstructed plan (Reconstruction by T. Riley, drawing by Y. Yee, Skidmore, Owings & Merrill)

"German Painting and Sculpture," The Museum of Modern Art, New York, 12 March – 26 April 1931. View of "corner wall" installation

"German Painting and Sculpture," The Museum of Modern Art, New York, 12 March – 26 April 1931. View of main gallery installation

thick walls are precisely the sort of massive construction that Barr disparaged elsewhere. The overall heaviness was compounded by the decision to chamfer the corners of the galleries, presumably to provide more continuous wall surfaces. These "corner walls" were used in almost every exhibition as surfaces for paintings. Screen walls were also constructed in front of the building's north-facing windows to provide additional window space.[5] As "functional" as the corner walls appear, they contribute to the impression of the museum as a sequence of highly defined, figural spaces.

The barely suppressed Beaux-Arts character of the galleries is further enhanced by the ceiling designs. All of the major rooms have biaxially symmetrical ceiling plans which incorporate the building's structural beams and a series of secondary, nonstructural beams designed to support light fixtures. As with classical ceiling moldings, the ceiling patterns are progressively more complex from the lesser to the more important rooms.

The doorways are for the most part arranged on axes and traditionally conceived as framed openings in the walls. The wall surfaces themselves are covered in a roughly woven, "warm beige"-colored linen called "monk's cloth."[6] Beyond a simple base and picture rail no moldings appear on the wall surfaces or around doorways. The lack of vertical articulation gives an overall horizontal reading to the spaces, though this "modern" conception of space is only faintly expressed.

The furnishings in the original galleries are evident in a number of the installation photos. The larger gallery has upholstered settees with wooden legs, and all of the galleries have "pale grey" chenille carpeting.[7]

"Cezanne, Gaugin, Seurat and Van Gogh,"
The Museum of Modern Art, New York,
7 November – 7 December 1929.
Foyer installation view

Unfortunately, there are not sufficient photos to reconstruct the entire plan, particularly the areas along the public corridor to the south. No photos of the library or offices exist. It is interesting to note, however, that Barr felt it important to include a room for books, especially as exhibition space was at such a premium. The program was eventually expanded to include the selling of books, and both subsequent homes of the museum, the townhouse and the current building at 11 West 53rd Street, have had a bookstore and library. Far from being imposing, the first galleries were accessed by a sixteen-by-sixteen-foot foyer with a sofa and reception desk.

To return to the question of authorship: Barr was certainly not a disinterested client; he presumably had an active role in the design. Lindeberg was probably drawn in due to his social stature rather than any perceived sympathy for progressive design. In addition to other expensive country homes, he designed the Pocantico Hills residence of James Stillman (both of Stillman's daughters were married to William Rockefeller's sons). Lindeberg's work before and after the museum project bears little affinity to the work in question and is, expectedly, heavily influenced by his years as an apprentice in the office of McKim, Mead and White. The galleries' Beaux-Arts-inspired *parti* most likely reflects his efforts. The balance of the scheme might be then seen as Lindeberg's half-hearted attempt to be "modern" under Barr's critical but unpracticed patronage.

Were others involved? Did Hitchcock have a role in the museum's design? As Helen Searing has argued, it is apparent that Hitchcock acted as an adviser to A. Everett Austin Jr. in the design of Austin's office at the Wadsworth Athenaeum.[8] But comparison of the two projects reveals little, if any, similarity.

Key to installation plan

Le Corbusier
1. Villa Savoye – exterior view
2. Villa Savoye – interior view
3. De Besteigui Penthouse
4. Villa Stein
5. Swiss Dormitory
6. Double Villa

J.J.P. Oud
7. Stuttgart Row
8. Shop – Hook of Holland
9. Housing – Hook of Holland
10. Housing – Kiefhoek
11. Church – Kiefhoek

Frank Lloyd Wright
12. Roberts House
13. Robie House
14. Taliesin
15. Millard House
16. Jones House
17. Jones House – aerial

Mies van der Rohe
18. Johnson Apartment
19. Lange House
20. Barcelona Pavilion
21. Tugendhat House – interior view
22. Tugendhat House – exterior view

Walter Gropius
23. Fagus Factory
24. Bauhaus Director's House
25. Bauhaus – general view
26. Bauhaus – second floor plan
27. Bauhaus – ground floor plan
28. Bauhaus Workshop and Classrooms
29. Dessau Employment Office
30. Dessau-Torten Housing

Bowman Brothers
31. Business Block – perspective
32. Architects' Offices – interior view

33. Apartment House – perspective
34. Prefabricated House – perspective

Howe & Lescaze
35. Chrystie-Forsyth – terrace plan
36. Chrystie-Forsyth – typical unit plan
37. Chrystie-Forsyth – ground floor plan
38. Translux Theater
39. F. V. Storrs – interior view
40. Oak Lane Country Day School
41. Hessian Hills – exterior view

42. Hessian Hills – exterior view
43. PSFS Tower

Housing Section
44 & 45. "Slum-Superslum"
46 & 47. "Slum Improvement"
48. Rothenberg Housing – site plan
49. Rothenberg Housing – aerial view
50. Rothenberg Housing – street view
51. Römerstadt Housing – aerial view
52 & 53. Radburn, N.J.
54 & 55. Typical Block – Sunnyside Gardens

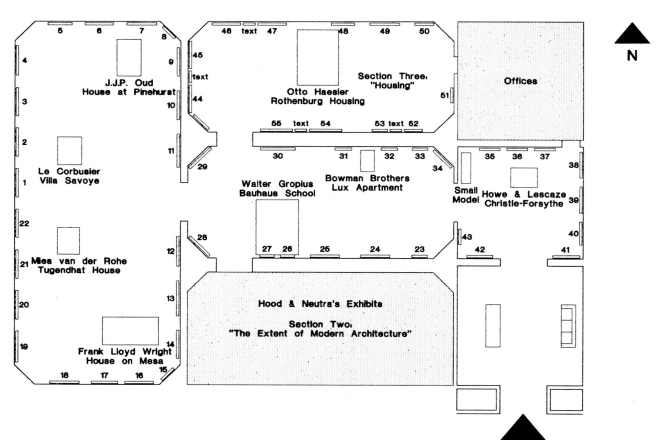

68

"Modern Architecture – International Exhibition," The Museum of Modern Art, New York, 10 February – 23 March 1932. Installation plan (reconstruction by T. Riley, drawing by Y. Yee and N. Katz, Skidmore, Owings & Merrill)

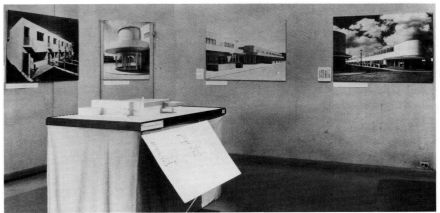

"Modern Architecture—International Exhibition," The Museum of Modern Art, New York,
10 February–23 March 1932. View of work by J.J.P. Oud

"Modern Architecture—International Exhibition," The Museum of Modern Art, New York,
10 February–23 March 1932. View of work by Frank Lloyd Wright

The Installation Plan

"Modern Architecture – International Exhibition,"
The Museum of Modern Art, New York,
10 February – 23 March 1932. View of work
by Howe & Lescaze

Most of the curators' decisions discussed heretofore have been in regard to the evolution of Exhibition 15's media and content. The exhibition's design adds to the matrix of decisions reflected in its ultimate presentation. The most significant curatorial decisions involved the positioning of the three sections within the museum's galleries and, further, positioning the nine architects within the galleries devoted to Section One. The existing galleries have definite hierarchical structure: the Entrance Room[9] and rooms A and C are the most important galleries and are arranged in an axial sequence. Clearly the most honorific of these spaces is Room C, situated at the end of the principal axis and much larger than the other rooms. Of the two remaining galleries on the principal axis, the Entrance Room also has a certain honorific distinction, experienced first and clearly visible from the entryway and foyer. The central gallery on the principal axis, Room A, is more of a transitional space, leading to the secondary galleries: Room B to the north and rooms D and E to the south.

A post-installation memo and the seven extant installation photographs (five of which have not been previously published) indicate the layout of the exhibition. In the main gallery, Room C, were positioned the exhibits of Le Corbusier, Mies, Wright, and Oud, establishing them as the most important architects in Section One. Of the four, Le Corbusier and Mies were given further distinction in that their exhibits were immediately to the right and left, respectively, of the principal axis and visible from the outer rooms. To underscore the importance of their work, the models of the Villa Savoye and the Tugendhat House had small electric lights attached to the model stands. The work of Howe & Lescaze was installed in the Entrance Room and the large model of the Chrystie-Forsyth project was placed opposite the entryway and foyer. The exhibits of Gropius and the Bowman Brothers were in the central gallery, Room A, the former closer to the main gallery.

"Modern Architecture - International Exhibition,"
The Museum of Modern Art, New York, 10
February – 23 March 1932. View of work by
Walter Gropius

The remaining exhibits in Section One, those of Hood and Neutra, were located in the least conspicuous gallery, Room D. All of the forty-one photographs in Section Two (The Extent of Modern Architecture) were displayed in the adjacent gallery, Room E. Similarly, all of the exhibits comprising Section Three (Housing section) were contained in a single gallery, Room B. The relatively less important positions of the second and third sections were predicted in the curators' statements throughout the exhibition development, specifically: "Distinct from the models, there are two sections which should be laid out so as to be more or less separate from the rest of the show."[10]

The selection of the Howe & Lescaze exhibit for the highly visible Entrance Room was logical. Their work was admired by Hitchcock, Johnson and Barr alike and the project presented in model form, the Chrystie-Forsyth Housing project, was considered strong. Additional factors, no doubt, played a role: the architects were from New York City and had been at the center of the *cause célèbre* created by the "Rejected Architects" exhibition the preceding year. They also fit the curator's profile of "movement" architects: they had considerable success in obtaining commissions including the recently completed PSFS skyscraper. Howe's critical writing for *T-Square,* renamed *Shelter* at the time of the exhibition, further added to his stature. The curators were also convinced of the feasibility of the Chrystie-Forsyth project and were committed to supporting it.

Mies's ascendancy did not diminish Le Corbusier, at least not in Hitchcock's opinion. (It may even be argued that Hitchcock preferred Le Corbusier and had reservations about Mies's extensive use of plate glass: he describes glass facades as "perhaps too fragile for *permanent* architecture."[11]) The preeminence of Mies and Le Corbusier is of no surprise, nor is the placement of Oud in the main gallery. The inclusion of Wright raises a number of questions, especially considering the exclusion of Gropius.

"Modern Architecture - International Exhibition,"
The Museum of Modern Art, New York,
10 February —23 March 1932. Model of Lux
Apartments by Bowman Brothers

If Wright was only reluctantly included in Exhibition 15, why was he featured in the main gallery? Perhaps the curators were genuinely enthusiastic about the House on the Mesa project, despite Wright's general historical position. Had his exhibit been positioned in the Entrance Room, it would have established a chronology corresponding to the curators' estimation of Wright as "a pioneer who is no longer to be imitated."[12] (Wright's projects do occupy that position in the catalogue, where the architects are presented by age.) However, considered collectively the main gallery exhibits suggest a number of interesting relationships. The fact that Wright, Mies, Le Corbusier and Oud are American, German, French and Dutch, respectively, supports the curatorial contention that "the style" was indeed an international (or at least transatlantic) phenomenon and not exclusively European. It is conceivable then that Howe & Lescaze could have been included in the *sanctus sanctorum* rather than Wright, considering their dual nationalities.

However, other relationships emerge. All of the projects showcased in model form within the main gallery were single-family residences, built or projected for wealthy clients with guest and servants' quarters. Not only was the House on the Mesa a "striking aesthetic statement of romantic expansiveness,"[13] it fit very neatly into the curators' attitude toward domestic luxury. Wright's plans call for a series of pavilion-type structures for living, sleeping and service, connected by loggias and cantilevered roofs. With a three-car garage, maids' rooms, a billiard room and an artificial lake cum swimming pool, the house was, in the midst of the Depression, more than a modest proposal. In the text panel that Wright supplied with the finished model, the building costs are projected at 125 thousand dollars (nearly twenty times the average cost of a home in 1931[14]).

Finally, and particularly in light of the curators' preference for European built works and American projected works, the models of the Tugendhat House and the Villa Savoye were placed opposite each other as were the models of the House for Pinehurst and the House on the Mesa. The two European projects occupying the more prominent positions were, of course, built works, in contrast to the two projected works for American clients: both a rebuke and an enticement to the American viewer.

The decision to exclude Gropius from the main gallery requires further discussion. If the arguments regarding the program dominated, Gropius's exclusion is rather straightforward. If international diversity was considered more important, Mies was the obvious choice to represent Germany over Gropius in the main gallery. The curators found Gropius a seminal figure among the "new pioneers" (see the earlier writings of Hitchcock and Barr). However, their positive remarks about his works frequently relate to his status as director of the much-admired Bauhaus. Mies's appointment to the directorship of the Bauhaus would only confirm their view of him as the most important architect in Germany.

While it remains a mystery how the Bowman Brothers retained their relatively important position in the exhibition without producing a single constructed building, it is further vexing that their exhibit was installed in the same room with that of Gropius. If proximity creates relationships, this pairing makes little sense, as it was done at the expense of both Neutra and Hood. The truly mediocre character of Hood's "Tower in the Country" may have determined his relatively obscure position.

But the curator's apparent preference of the Bowman Brothers' exhibit over that of Neutra is not as justifiable. Perhaps they did not want two school projects in one room. Perhaps the Bowman Brothers were chosen because, despite a worsening financial situation, they were able to present a fairly large commission that appeared to have some chance of being built. Neutra's Ring Plan School may have suffered in contrast from being a self-initiated, utopian proposition. It is also possible that the curators could not resist opposing Hood's tower with Neutra's scheme. (An underlying element of the Rush City proposals was a distinct anti-skyscraper ethos.)

The Installation Design

Despite hopes that Mies might come to New York to "arrange" the exhibition, Johnson spent a considerable amount of time planning how the installation would be designed. Before Johnson left for Europe in June 1931, the curators had already determined the size of the photo enlargements. Furthermore, in response to a series of questions regarding the installation design from Howe & Lescaze, Blackburn writes, "Before he [Johnson] left he set the maximum number of photographs at 50. . . . I know that Mr. Johnson wants to keep the Exhibition as a whole consistent as possible in design. Hence, I doubt that he would want each architect to design his individual layout of photographs."[15]

Even as Mies was being invited Johnson writes, "Explanatory plans, elevations and perspectives will be placed on the wall behind each model. Enlarged photographs of actual buildings by these architects will also be shown."[16] By and large, this is an accurate description of the installation of the exhibits in Section One. In this manner the model more or less acted to define the area of each architects' exhibit. Beyond this vague definition of territory, the installation design was, indeed, "consistent." In Johnson's words: "We will at least have a simple and understandable arrangement."[17] Johnson's comments were made in relating to Barr his impression of the Frank Lloyd Wright exhibition installed in the Prüssische Akademie der Kunst in Berlin by H. Th. Wijdeveld during the summer of 1931,[18] which Johnson refers to as "frightful." The Wijdeveld installation was organized around a series of tall freestanding partitions with "wings" on each end. On the partitions and on the walls of the exhibition hall were drawings and photos of varying scales, mounted salon-style. Models of varying scales and materials were placed asymmetrically in various locations. In contrast to this freely composed arrangement, Johnson's installation was the very model of stylistic "discipline" that the curators urged on American architects. In an ironic reference to classical architecture Johnson instructs that the photographs "be placed in a frieze around the rooms, allowing about 2 ft. in

"Modern Architecture - International Exhibtion," Cleveland Museum of Art, 27 October – 5 December 1932. View of Raymond Hood's work at right

"Modern Architecture - International Exhibition," Cleveland Museum of Art, 27 October – 5 December 1932. Installation view

between."[19] The uniformity of the media, the scale of the models and photographs, the spacing and the hanging height all contributed to a composed character.

Johnson's installation did not go unnoticed, particularly in New York City where viewers of architectural exhibitions were accustomed to salon-style installations, frequently on a grand scale.[20] Johnson had, no doubt, seen a number of these as well as exhibitions in Europe. He had also designed the "Rejected Architects" exhibition. There is little evidence that Johnson was influenced greatly by any of these experiences, although Exhibition 15's installation aspired to the simplicity of Mies's exhibition at the Deutscher Werkbund Austellung of 1931, which Johnson had seen. However, photographs of Barr's minimalist installations of fine art exhibitions suggest a more immediate model. Even the scale of Exhibition 15's photo enlargements was consistent with the scale of the post-impressionist works that Barr had championed in the museum's earlier exhibitions. While the media implied, first, an operation of surrogacy, the installation supports a secondary reading of the models and photographs as *objets d'art* in themselves. Johnson further instructs the subscribers that the photographs should be "hung in the same manner as paintings."

The presentation style was consistent throughout all three sections, though the format varied from section to section. In Section One the proposed presentation of elevations and perspectives never materialized though behind each model were placed photographs of "actual buildings by [the] architects." In general the sequence was chronological, with exceptions: the Villa Savoye and the Tugendhat House photographs were taken out of sequence and so appear behind the models of the same projects. Le Corbusier's Double House at Weissenhof was also taken out of sequence so that it would be adjacent to

Mies van der Rohe, Exhibition of Wood Veneers, Berlin Building Exhibition, 1931.

"Henri Matisse," The Museum of Modern Art, New York, 3 November - 6 December 1931. View of main gallery installation

Oud's Weissenhof project. The enlargements were typically three feet high[21] and hung with the center of the photograph at eye level. The widths varied from approximately two to five feet. The images were, of course, black and white reproductions, bled edge-to-edge and mounted on plywood without frames. Between the photographs were, with few exceptions, small prints of the plans of the projects. The curators' apparent unwillingness to diminish the importance of the photographs was at the expense of any readily legible reading of the plans. The heights and widths varied but typically were no greater than eight inches in either direction. Mounted flush with the bottom edge of the photographs, they are barely visible in the installation photos. The model bases were typically below the bottom edge of the photographs. With the exception of Wright's custom-designed base for the House on the Mesa, the models had extremely ill-conceived "skirts" of the same fabric as the wall covering. While the bases may have been low so as not to obscure the photographs, the curators were also thinking of the lay viewer. The plans were near the same scale as the models and mounted on easels attached to the stands or on the adjacent walls to allow the viewer to compare the roof silhouette to the plan at a glance. (Given the curators' aesthetic preoccupations, it is notable that Mies's seminal Barcelona Pavilion was not included in Exhibition 15 in model form. To convince Barr that Mies should design a new project for the exhibition, Johnson pointed out that the Barcelona Pavilion "would not be good for the purposes of the model since one would see nothing but the roof."[22] Barr, rather than suggesting a change in the base heights, rejected the Spanish project but insisted on using the Tugendhat House.)

An exception to the above-described formats was made for the Chrystie-Forsyth project. Facing the foyer, the raised model base put the model at eye level, and the two-foot-high prints were raised to be visible behind it. Six line-drawing perspectives, reproduced photographically to the same dimensions as

76

the half-tone photographs, were also shown. Wright, Hood and Howe & Lescaze also produced illustrated text panels for their models, and the last presented a site model as well as the larger model of the typical housing block.

Below the photographs and perspectives, and attached to the model bases, were sans serif labels with the name of the architect, the project and the dates of construction.[23]

Section Two (The Extent of Modern Architecture) also consisted principally of photographs, though smaller in size: uniformly fifteen inches high and ranging from eleven to thirty inches wide. They were hung in two "friezes" (five inches apart) with the upper row at eye level. The projects were presented by nationality, and placards with the names of the countries were mounted above each sequence. There were no plans of the forty-one projects presented in Section Two and only one line drawing. In a curious departure from the curators' established preference for "actual monuments" and projects that "have a chance of being built," a perspective of Frederick Kiesler's Guild Cinema "as projected" was presented adjacent to a photo of the same project "as built." With the exception of Nicolaiev & Firsenko, Mendelsohn and Lurçat, each architect exhibited only one project in Section Two. Only Otto Haesler and Ernst May were represented elsewhere in the exhibition. Unfortunately, no installation photos exist of "The Extent of Modern Architecture."

Section Three shared the uniform appearance of the rest of the exhibition. All of the eleven photographs, three of the text panels and the one site plan were three feet high, the same format as in Section One. A fourth text panel introducing the exhibit was slightly larger. In distinction to the other two sections, the housing exhibit was more explicitly didactic and the text panels were an integral component of the installation. Three texts dealt with different

"Modern Architecture—International Exhibition,"
The Museum of Modern Art, New York,
10 February – 23 March 1932. Housing section
installation; model of Rothenberg Housing
Development by Otto Haesler in foreground

aspects of housing and were framed, in a sort of triptych, by two photographs:
"Slum-Superslum" compared the densities of the Upper and Lower East Side,
"Long Island City" compared a crowded jumble of rear yards with Sunnyside
Gardens by Clarence Stein and Henry Wright and "Slum Improvement"
compared aerial views of J.J.P. Oud's Kiefhoek Housing Project and the
Amalgamated Grand Street Apartments. While the housing section had the
"look" of the rest of the exhibition, the enlarged text panels challenged the "fine
art" presentation favored elsewhere by the curators. Whether this was
Johnson's or the RPAA members' idea isn't clear, but the result certainly
presented "vague theories" as the equivalent to the "actual monuments."
Unfortunately, the text panels are badly documented; only one of them is legible
in the installation photos and also appears to have been published elsewhere.[24]

As in Section One, the exhibit was organized around a model: in this instance
Haesler's enormous (four-by-eight-foot) maquette of the Rothenberg *Siedlung*.
Hung on the wall adjacent to the model were a site plan and two photographs.

"Modern Architecture—International Exhibition," Cleveland Museum of Art, 27 October – 5 December 1932. Model of Chrystie-Forsyth Housing Development by Howe & Lescaze in foreground; missing text and photograph beyond (Model and drawings at left were not in New York exhibition view)

Photographs

From the outset the curators consistently refer to Exhibition 15 as an exhibition of models, despite the fact that by the time it was installed it would have been more accurate to call it a photographic exhibition. While the models may have attracted more attention, especially from the public, the photo enlargements at eye level dominated.

The dividing line between artifact and surrogate lay in their authorship. As was the custom of the day, no credits were given for the photographers. Neither Hitchcock not Barr were accomplished photographers. Johnson owned a hand-machined camera, but there is no evidence to suggest that he took any of the photographs in the exhibition. All three collected photographs assiduously for their publications and records. In his publications Hitchcock generally acknowledges the sources of the photographs—frequently the architects rather than the photographers. Only a few photographs (e.g., Johnson requested that Neutra rephotograph the Lovell House to show more mature vegetation[25]) can be considered as having been taken specifically for the exhibition.

Architectural photography was then, as now, considered a technical sub-specialty. The photographers were not considered the authors of their work. Nevertheless, the names of a number of the photographers are known,[26] as many of the photographs in Exhibition 15, despite the assertions of the curators to the contrary,[27] had previously been published in architectural magazines. Like other periodicals that had come to rely on photographers for their viability, architectural magazines more conscientiously credited the photographers' efforts.

The work of dozens of photographers was represented in the exhibition. A good number of the enlargements were printed in Germany; the others were produced in the New York photo studio of William Seidman. All of the enlargements were made from prints rather than from negatives, as the curators did not want the architects to risk sending the latter (often glass rather than film)

79

Clauss & Daub, Filling Station, 1931.
Unaltered exterior view

through the mail. In some instances variations in technique and/or quality are evident and objectionable. For the most part, however, a certain consistency to the work reigns, due in part to the editing and preferences of the curators and in other instances to the prevailing norms of architectural documentation. The majority of the photographs are closely framed exterior shots of the buildings taken from an angle that emphasizes the architecture as an isolated mass.

With the exception of few interiors, the buildings are daylit and the photos taken at eye level. Except in the urban shots, there is little sign of human presence; the baby carriage on the Millard House terrace and the pack of cigarettes in the Bowman Brothers interior are rare exceptions.

Within these parameters the photographs reveal a certain objective detachment consistent with the curators' attitudes toward architecture. The close framing of the images and the cropping of contextual material contribute to the minimalist installation. While it could be argued that this was the custom of the day and that the curators simply printed the images they received, the consistency suggests heavy editing. In the instance of Clauss & Daub's filling station, the curators altered the photographs to remove an apparently offending Victorian house.

The exceptions to these general rules are frequently the more interesting photographs: the San Sebastian Yacht Club, the Lovell House and House on Lago Maggiore are all portrayed within their surrounding landscapes. Similarly, the urban context adds to the image of the PSFS tower, and the aerial views of the large housing projects add a dimension entirely missing in the eye-level photographs. For the Villa Savoye, Tugendhat House and Hessian Hills School the combination of interior and exterior views begins to capture the spatial qualities of the projects, which are given little consideration elsewhere in the exhibition and the book and catalogue. Likewise, the few interior projects presented invariably focus on furniture rather than on spatiality.

Models

The makers of the professionally built maquettes, with the exception of the Villa Savoye model, are unknown.[28] Regardless of Johnson's prediction that the models would become "invaluable as historical documents" (he was right), the whereabouts of most of them are unknown.

As might be expected, the materials employed in the models varied extensively, despite Johnson's original request that they be constructed of cardboard. Oud's House for Pinehurst is the simplest: completely monochromatic and made of a single material (cardboard), it provides no indication of the interior or of details extraneous to the architecture. Similarly abstract are the models of the Bowman Brothers and Neutra projects, both crafted in aluminum. All of the other models are polychromatic, using various combinations of wood, papier-mâché, glass and, in the case of the Tugendhat House model, chrome and marble. While the Villa Savoye, the Bauhaus School and the House on the Mesa models have perceivable interiors, the popular press remarked primarily on the scale furniture, trees, and automobiles of Mies's model. The principal logistical difficulties with the installation were related to the models. Despite Johnson's exhortations that they be professionally built and crated, more than half of the models were severely damaged in shipping.

Openings

Throughout the exhibition planning the curators managed to compartmentalize the Industrial section, representing techno-functional concerns as important though clearly separate and secondary. Nevertheless, as the exhibition developed there was no discernible lack of enthusiasm for the section's remaining component: housing. This enthusiasm may have been spurred by Howe and Lescaze's Chrystie-Forsyth proposal, which was featured in the exhibition "preview" on 29 January 1932. In addition to younger architects, the event's invitees were mostly housing technocrats, bankers, builders and real estate developers. Many had already lent their names to a second list of the exhibition supporters appearing in the catalogue as "Patrons Who Have Advanced the Study of Housing."[29] A general invitation was also extended to President Hoover's Home Ownership and Home Building Conference recently convened to address the nation's housing crisis. Clark, the exhibition committee secretary, personally wrote to Hoover: "It is the sincere belief of the Museum that the Exhibition of Modern Architecture will exert a most beneficial influence on architecture and building in the United States and particularly in the field of multiple dwelling developments both urban and suburban."[30]

In addition to mentioning the Chrystie-Forsyth project in the preview's invitation, the museum sent out a separate press release on that project alone, and Barr wrote letters on Howe & Lescaze's behalf to various governmental and financial interests. Despite these efforts, the preview was not well-attended. In Bauer's words: "No really Big Shots were there and Messrs. Hitchcock-Barr-Johnson were uncomfortably nervous."[31] The official opening, held on February 9, was more of a social event and, judging by the press coverage, more of a success. However, there was one notable absence: Johnson became ill from exhaustion and spent several nights in an East Side hospital.

The opening was not the last of Exhibition 15's public events. On February 19 an Architects' Symposium was attended by a good number of New York architects. The evening as planned by Barr was to be informal and consist of a number of short presentations by Hitchcock, Harvey Wiley Corbett, Hood, Howe, Mumford and others.[32]

Howe's brief presentation was listed as "Why I Turned from Conservative to Modern Architecture." In addition to his talents, which the curators appreciated, Howe became an important figure in the International Style propaganda campaign due to his age and his previous stature as a mainstream historicist architect. The title of his talk suggests a confessional tract, and the inclusion of an example of his traditional work in the catalogue was certainly intended as an example of "conservative architects the world over turning to modern architecture."

As noted above, the evenhandedness of the International Style project ebbed and flowed throughout its year of planning. While the catalogue added a polemical edge to the exhibition that could not have been inferred from the prospectus *Built To Live In*, the Architects' Symposium was more egalitarian in composition. As might be expected, Hitchcock spoke on the International Style. However, Royal Cortissoz (who would write an extremely negative review of the exhibition in the *New York Herald Tribune*)[33] was invited to provide a conservative rebuttal. Cortissoz declined to attend but when the proceedings of the symposium were published in *Shelter* magazine various other critics were offered a chance to articulate opposing viewpoints.[34]

While the curators elsewhere attempted to compartmentalize Mumford's message, there appears to have been no scripting in the symposium. Barr requested that Mumford speak of "the architect's responsibility in housing."[35]

Furthermore, he urged Mumford to "make it fairly aggressive for certainly American architects have been painfully neglectful of the housing question in America." Mumford's short presentation was, indeed, aggressive. To the architects assembled he put the questions:

> *Do you still think this [housing] problem can be solved by one clever technical dodge or another, or have you sufficient intelligence to see that it must be treated as an organic whole? Are you ready to help organize mass-production? Are you familiar with the latest examples of community design, from Frankfurt-am-Main to Radburn? Are you ready to abandon the worn out theories of individual design and ornament that were fastened on your architectural education: can you think and design in rational wholes?*[36]

More heavily attended than the Architects' Symposium was the Decorators' Meeting held on March 14. Organized in conjunction with various organizations such as the American Institute of Interior Decorators, the evening's main feature was a lecture by Johnson entitled "Interior Decoration vs. Interior Architecture."[37]

Critical and General Reception

In his foreword to the 1966 edition of *The International Style* Hitchcock refers to the project as a *succes d'estime*,[38] an evaluation perhaps colored by hindsight. Johnson's contemporaneous characterization of the exhibition's reception is less positive:

> *I may safely say that there was not one really critical review of the Exhibition. For the most part the critics make excerpts from the catalogue, or if they are constitutionally opposed to modern architecture, they merely remark that the Exhibition displeases them.*[39]

Johnson's remarks confirm Stern, Gilmartin and Mellin's views as expressed in *New York 1930*.[40] There was neither broad coverage of the event nor notable attendance as compared to other contemporary architectural exhibitions in New York City. Some thirty-three thousand people viewed Exhibition 15 during the six weeks it was open to the public. In contrast, 186 thousand people attended the Metropolitan Museum of Art's 1929 "The Architect and the Industrial Arts" exhibition. Exhibition 15's critical reception, also mentioned in *New York 1930* and documented in Suzanne Stephens's research,[41] was similarly faint and, for the most part, predictable: critics supportive of modern architecture reacted positively; critics who preferred more traditional architecture were, by and large, unenthusiastic.

If the critical reverberations were disappointing, the general press's reaction was even more so. Supporting Catherine Bauer's assessment that the exhibition had made housing "safe for millionaires,"[42] the following appeared in the *Hartford Courant*:

> *An exhibition of advanced housing models, made of little pieces of metal, glass, and wood, will be opened Saturday afternoon, April 20, with a tea to the members of the Wadsworth Athenaeum.*[43]

Given the curators' emphasis on the models as *objets*, the press's fascination with the "miniature apartment dwellings" is not surprising, nor is it limited to the housing projects. Even A. Everett Austin, quoted in the popular press, makes similar comments regarding Mies's model:

> The model of the Tugendhat House in Brno, Czechoslovakia, included in the exhibition is actually furnished with miniature pieces of metal furniture. . . . [The models] are extremely delicate and difficult to transport.[44]

The models produced an unexpected response, as did the emphasis on the single-family residence, which created a level of familiarity that encouraged what might be called domestic criticism. Another reporter provided the following observation for general readership: "Incidentally, there are usually no cellars in the house of the International Style, and the attic is eliminated by providing elsewhere for storage space."[45]

The preceding, excerpted from Wright's more comprehensive philosophy of the home, hardly portended the stylistic Armageddon envisioned by the curators. Perhaps most disappointing, however, was the apparent inability of the critics and general public to discern the finely wrought stylistic messages of Exhibition 15. Barr, Hitchcock and Johnson might have been shocked to find how loosely their connoisseurial statement was interpreted. A reporter for the Worcester, Mass. *Sunday Telegram* (who also referred to "Miss van der Rohe, famous German draftsman") wrote that Hood's Tower in the Country project "well exemplifies the theory held by most modern architects that rural districts are best for skyscraper homes."[46] Yet another surprising observation was: "The most extreme development of the International Style which has yet been suggested is the Dymaxion House, proposed but not yet built by Buckminster Fuller."[47]

Only within the architectural community did the exhibition cause extended debate. As Hitchcock describes it, "As the epithets fly about my own head. . . . I can only recall the British battles over the Houses of Parliament and the Government Offices in Whitehall."[48] Much of the criticism centered on the curators' formulation of the International Style, which even Oud (who generally supported the curators) referred to as "school mastering."[49] The emigre California architect Rudolph Schindler was more explicit:

> I am not a stylist, functionalist, nor any other sloganist. Each of my buildings deals with a different architectural problem, the existence of which has been entirely forgotten in this period of rational mechanization. The questions of whether a house is really a house is more important to me than the fact it is made of steel, glass, putty or hot air.[50]

The foregoing is from a letter in which Schindler asks, rather undiplomatically, to be included in the Los Angeles venue of the exhibition. Even as Schindler and others sought to be included, Wright insisted on being taken out. In addition to the misunderstandings regarding the models, photographs and drawings, Wright was displeased with various aspects of the exhibition and the publicity surrounding it: the curators' unfavorable comments in the catalogue as well as reports of disparaging remarks made by Hood about Wright's work. Wright cabled Johnson:

MY WAY HAS BEEN TOO LONG AND TOO LONELY TO MAKE A BELATED BOW AS A MODERN ARCHITECT IN COMPANY WITH A SELF ADVERTISING AMATEUR AND A HIGH POWERED SALESMAN NO BITTERNESS AND SORRY BUT KINDLY AND FINALLY DROP ME OUT OF YOUR PROMOTION[51]

Mumford attempted to persuade Wright to reverse his decision and eventually he did so on the condition that the curators print his essay "Of Thee I Sing" and make it available at the exhibition.[52] As a compromise, the curators included it in the special issue of *Shelter* magazine devoted to the exhibition and provided copies for the public during the exhibition's tour.[53]

In addition to Wright's essay and the transcripts of the Architects' Symposium, three opposing viewpoints by K. Lonberg-Holm, Arthur T. North and Chester Aldrich were printed in the magazine.[54] Lonberg-Holm's critique consists of excerpting all of the curators' references to "style" in the catalogue and juxtaposing them with an advertisement for toilet fixtures and Mies's manifesto from the magazine *G* wherein he rejects "all aesthetic speculation," "all dogma" and "all formalism." North's and Aldrich's critiques a similarly negative, the former titled "Old New Stuff" and the latter "Modernism and Publicity." Aldrich's architectural partner William Adams Delano adds to the criticism in a subsequent issue of *Shelter*: "After centuries of struggle to evolve a culture worthy of his position in the animal kingdom, is this to be man's end? No better, no worse than the insects, ants and caterpillars."[55]

On March 23 Exhibition 15 closed and the material was crated for shipment to Philadelphia.

Notes on the Chronology of
The International Style

Two additional issues should be addressed, as they figure prominently in the anecdotal histories of Exhibition 15. Sixty years after the fact it is difficult, if not impossible, to determine who might have been the first to use the term International Style as we understand it today. It is apparent that the term had some currency with Barr, Hitchcock and Johnson from 1928 onward. Nevertheless, the significance of their various citations is not always clear.

Use of the term international relative to things modern, particularly architecture, was not unusual by the middle of the 1920s, as evidenced in numerous publications such as Hilberseimer's *Internationale Neue Baukunst* and Gropius's *Internationale Architektur*.[1] In the broadest sense, emphasis on the "international" was an implicit criticism of nationalist policies, both cultural and political. Conversely, if modernists saw things international as having an inherently positive character over things national, imbued the word with equally negative associations derived principally from right-wing opposition to the avowed international mission of the socialist and pacifist movements as well as fascism's paranoid obsessions with "international Jewish conspiracies," a staple of anti-Semitic propaganda.

Linking "international" with "style" has, of course, additional meanings. It was Hitchcock who first used the term in print (in his article "Four Harvard Architects" published in *The Hound and Horn* in 1928). Even so, his usage is less definitive than the one that Barr, Hitchcock and Johnson would adopt later, and the term is modified by the indefinite article: an international style.[2]

Some of the anecdotal history of the term should be mentioned. Calvin Tomkins in a 1987 essay on Johnson writes, "Barr coined the term two years before [the exhibition]."[3] Tomkins is probably referring to Barr's 1929 characterization of Moise Ginsberg's work as representing "that international style of which

Le Corbusier, Gropius and Oud are perhaps the first masters."[4] In this instance Barr's use of the term was most likely a simple matter of description rather than a conscious coining of a new phrase. Hitchcock's use of the term in Modern Architecture (1929) is similarly unself-conscious (although both authors use the definitive article) and appears only once in the entire book.[5]

In a lecture given thirty years after Exhibition 15 Johnson recalls, "Alfred Barr and Henry-Russell Hitchcock used the phrase in 1931 when we were all searching for a name for the obviously clear line of work being done in the 20's."[6] Elsewhere Johnson claims, "[Barr] coined the phrase, Russell Hitchcock wrote the book and I was the drummer and screamer-arounder."[7] Barr, in his preface to the Hitchcock-Johnson book, writes, "The authors have called it [the new modern style] the International Style."[8] In his research and interviews for Good Old Modern, Russell Lynes arrived at less certain conclusions: "It is not clear, even in the minds of Barr and Hitchcock and Johnson, which of them was responsible for the phrase 'International Style.'"[9]

In an October 1930 letter to Johnson Haesler refers to Hitchcock and Johnson's working title: "The New International Style, 1922–1932."[10] This is certainly more self-conscious than any other previous usage and suggests a specific body of work. Furthermore, as modified by the word "new," the title suggests a direct reference to existing art historical nomenclature: the International Style of painting that appeared in France, the Netherlands and Italy before the Renaissance.

Hitchcock does not use the modifier "new" again. As Haesler cites a title and employs an existing term that was normally capitalized, the use of uppercase initials is slightly obscured. Hitchcock contends in the 1966 foreword to the second edition of The International Style that it was Barr not he or Johnson who first capitalized and therefore solemnized the phrase."[11] In the book Hitchcock uses the phrase with lowercase initials throughout the text while Barr uses uppercase initials in the preface. Nevertheless, the book appeared nearly a year after Johnson used the phrase with uppercase initials in his article on the New School in *The Arts* and in other publications.[12] Yet at this time Johnson frequently capitalized key words (Exhibition, Show, Building Exposition, Siedlungen, American Architecture, Architectural Show, etc.) in his correspondence and texts. Elsewhere in *The Arts* article he also capitalizes "the New Style" and in a letter to Mumford refers to the "International Group."

Who, then, first used the phrase? It is probably safe to say that Hitchcock first employed it in the general sense use today. These early citations, with the indefinite article and in conjunction with existing nomenclature, indicate a certain hesitancy about its legitimacy, however, and it could be argued that its wide currency is due to Barr's and Johnson's affirmative use of the term, with uppercase initials and without direct reference to its historic antecedent.

It is also useful to consider at what point the project, which had been conceived as a publication, expanded to include plans for an exhibition. As with many of the details of the chronology of Exhibition 15, Hitchcock's and Johnson's subsequent recollections of this time are frequently contradictory. Johnson suggests in his 1982 interview with Peter Eisenman that Barr asked him to direct the exhibition in the fall of 1929,[13] to which Wodehouse appears to refer when he states that Johnson became director of the Department of Architecture in 1929. Hitchcock is less certain in his interviews for Lynes's *Good Old Modern*:

> Whether I had been approached before this [summer 1930] I don't know—perhaps informally. At any rate, it was far enough along so it was decided that Philip and I were to do it, to pool our knowledge of European international-style architecture, and we were to go and collect the material."[14]

However, in the forward to the 1966 edition of The International Style Hitchcock's brief history of the curatorial planning states that the project, both book and exhibition, was initiated in 1931.

It is implausible that Barr suggested, as Johnson recounts in the interview, an actual exhibition as early as the fall of 1929. At that time Johnson was a member of the Museum's Junior Advisory Committee and not director of the Department of Architecture. In August of that year Barr was preparing a pamphlet on the new museum suggesting that their would "probably" be a department of architecture (as well as photography, typography, industrial design, decorative arts, furniture, drawings, prints and films) sometime in the future.[15] The trustees were more cautious about Barr's ambitious plans and edited his text to read more vaguely: "In time the museum would expand . . . to include other phases of modern art." As the museum began to define itself it is clear that the trustees were interested in emphasizing painting and sculpture over anything else.

Hitchcock's recollection that the project was proposed in 1930 and that he and Johnson went to Europe that summer with the express purpose of collecting material for the exhibition is equally implausible. As Johnson's letters indicate, their trip developed a specific purpose only after Hitchcock (already in Europe) decided to rewrite Modern Architecture. Prior to that Johnson's planned itinerary was much shorter and involved a month in Paris to learn French.[16]

Perhaps Barr suggested the exhibition when the three met in Hamburg, but again it is implausible that Johnson, who related countless details of his trip to his mother and was very much eager to demonstrate his competence, would fail to mention such a momentous turn of events. Furthermore, while Johnson was in Berlin he made tentative arrangements to attend the university there, going as far as meeting with a faculty member and filling out matriculation forms.[17] It seems unlikely that Johnson would have gone to these efforts if Barr had asked him to mount an exhibition at the museum.

Hitchcock's 1966 account, which places the book's and the exhibition's inception in 1931, is also unlikely, as Haesler's letter suggests that the book had a working title by September 1930 and that Goodyear had the curators' proposal in hand by December of the same year.

The confusion in the curators' mind is caused, no doubt, by the fact that from the time they met Barr had plans for an architectural exhibition and may very well have suggested at a very early date that Hitchcock and Johnson be involved. However, the evidence strongly suggests that discussions about a specific exhibition, based on Hitchcock's book-in-progress, began in New York only in the fall of 1930.

Afterword

How the International Style eventually became a *succès d'estime* after its relatively inauspicious beginnings is beyond the scope of this essay. Hopefully future scholars will analyze the project's critical trajectory over the intervening sixty years. In conclusion, some critical questions and tentative answers can be proposed.

The research presented here may suggest that the process by which the International Style became a *succes d'estime* may have also altered and expanded its definition, to the point where contemporary conceptions of the curators' program bear little resemblance to their positions of 1932. For example, consider Vincent Scully's use of the term in his 1985 essay "Buildings Without Souls."[1] In one instance he refers to the "International Style slab in its empty plaza" to describe the speculative office buildings derived from Mies's Seagram Building. This degraded building type, with its utter lack of formal character, is thus associated with a style that expressed, at best, a marked ambivalence about skyscrapers and was frequently criticized as overly concerned with aesthetics.

Any critical reevaluation must necessarily question the various additions to, and reductions of, the curator's positions of 1932. The enduring objections to Exhibition 15 by those sympathetic to the modernist project claim that the curators stripped European modernism of its ideological component even as they propagandized its formal aspects in the United States. Hitchcock's 1932 defense against such criticism is pertinent:

> There are . . . *several intellectually valid critical attitudes which should be perpetually brought before the general public. The technical attitude . . . is particularly effective in a country governed by a great engineer* [Hoover]. *The attitude of the sociologist must*

*appeal to everyone in so far as he is a social unit and feels a duty
to ameliorate the condition of other men. . . . The attitude of those
. . . who distrust the American passion for mere fashionable
novelties and stress the evolutionary continuity of modern
architecture is a necessary corrective. . . . Even the aesthetic
attitude, which assumes that the best modern architecture
achieves a beauty of form at once new and intense, might be
encouraged to continue to express itself. . . . Since the last is my
own attitude, I suppose however much I may desire to fuse it with
something of the other above mentioned attitudes, I must defend it
at least pragmatically for itself.*[2]

It is useful to scrutinize Hitchcock's stated desire to "fuse" aesthetics with
related technical, sociological and cultural issues. Yet to do so requires a
better understanding of his formal position than is common today. In addition to
"International Style slabs in their empty plazas," Mies's other post-1932 work,
such as the low-rise IIT campus, is also frequently cited as exemplifying the
International Style, despite the fact that those works bear little resemblance to
most of the works presented in the exhibition and despite evidence that
Hitchcock was unconvinced of the appropriateness of the widespread use of
glass in "permanent" architecture.

The International Style is now characterized not only by Mies's post-exhibition
innovations but equally and alternately by Le Corbusier's pre-1932 works. H. H.
Arnason's *History of Modern Art*,[3] written for general readership, is
symptomatic: of the illustrations in the chapter on the International Style, the
greatest number are of works by Le Corbusier, three of which (the Villa Savoye,
the Weissenhof villas and the Swiss Pavilion) were included in the 1932
exhibition. When Scully in 1985 describes the International Style as "abstract

and avant-garde" and to its qualities as "linearity and thinness," he is referring to these archetypal projects by Le Corbusier.

Neither Mies's post-exhibition production nor Le Corbusier's work of the 1920s fully represents the variety of work presented in 1932. Hitchcock's inclusion of Le Corbusier's de Mandrot House and the porter's lodge at Villa Savoye (both rubble-walled), the plywood Finnish Pavilion for the Antwerp Exposition of 1930, the Aluminaire House, and Otto Eisler's House for Two Brothers (which had a cementitious finish with red stone aggregate) suggests that the curator had a far broader conception of the physical and constructive characteristics of the International Style than is now supposed.

If this heterogeneity was lost as the International Style became associated with the cliches of postwar commercial architecture, the subtlety of Hitchcock's overall critical position, as stated in his 1932 defense of the International Style, was also obscured. Hitchcock's technical "attitude" may not be evident in "International Style slabs in their empty plazas," yet it is hard to disassociate the van Nelle Factory, the Aluminaire House and Figini & Pollini's Electrical House from their techno-functional sources, even within Hitchcock's aesthetic framework.

The programmatic message of the exhibition reflects what Hitchcock describes as the "sociological attitude" and the position of those who "distrust the American passion for mere fashionable novelty." The latter reveals Hitchcock's classicizing conservatism, which as much as any political considerations contributed to the exhibition's blatant appeals to the status quo. In addition to privileging the single-family house and the cultural biases that it represented was the separate but distinct programmatic message of the various other building types presented in the exhibition and the book: Residence for Single

Women, German Metal Worker's Union Building, the Open Air School and others, including the large number of social housing projects. The inclusion of these varied building types and the new social structures they implied suggested a link between modern aesthetics and the possibility of a radically different culture. This relatively undefined bonding of formal and ideological attitudes proved resilient. Decades later, revisionist theoreticians seized the image of the 1972 demolition of the Pruitt-Igoe housing development as a virtual emblem of their post-modernist critique. While any number of aesthetically banal buildings might have served this purpose, the program—social housing—was crucial. Ironically, the International Style remained, for over forty years, linked with the very ideological basis that it purportedly denied.

Hitchcock in his 1932 defense of Exhibition 15 outlines an idealistic conception of a robust forum wherein "several intellectually valid critical attitudes" act as competing and counterbalancing forces in shaping the new architecture, a view resulting from Hitchcock's liberal university education. His personal position within this construction as outspoken defender of the "aesthetic attitude" was distorted by his perceptions of the Neue Sachlichkeit and its claim to offer an objective, anti-aesthetic architecture. Present-day conceptions of the International Style are colored more by an after-the-fact hardening of the curators' positions along Hitchcock's supposed critical demarcations than by the variety of positions presented by Hitchcock, Barr, Johnson and Mumford in Exhibition 15.

This essay is not an apologia for the International Style, and certainly not for the International Style as it has come to be seen by Scully and others. Rather, the intention has been to suggest, first, that current conceptions of the International Style are not necessarily related to the actual positions of the curators in 1932 and, second, that the intervening transformations and eventual degradation of the critical material presented in Exhibition 15 are not necessarily linked to a flaw in its critical position. Any subsequent critical reevaluation of the trajectory of the International Style should move beyond Exhibition 15 itself and engage the cultural forces that produced the latter-day manifestations of the "International Style": speculative real estate development, the corporate character (of both clients and architects) of postwar America, the ubiquity of the automobile and the ongoing conflict between individual and collective ideologies.

The timeliness of such an evaluation is obvious as we find ourselves in a world bearing striking similarities to the cultural conditions of 1932: worldwide economic instability, a severe housing crisis, and an architectural culture obsessed with simulation. It will be a great historical loss if the current crisis spurs an unconsidered reformulation of prewar modernist values as a sort of architectural hairshirt to be worn after the excesses of the past decade. In the same vein, the cultural and political vagaries of the late twentieth century should not discourage the continued adaptation of the critical visions of radical modernism.

The appearance of the Black Death style of painting in mid-fourteenth century Italy, after the initial manifestations of the Renaissance, is roughly analogous to our contemporary situation. This particular artistic expression involved a drastic reorientation of Florentine and Siennese painting away from the experimentation of the early Renaissance and toward the historical, hierarchical models of the Middle Ages. The formal qualities of the Black Death style are incomprehensible apart from the political and social forces that created it: the collapse of the Florentine banking system, civil war and repeated outbreaks of the bubonic plague.

Given the volatility of our own social structures, beset by a contemporary plague, banking failures and political upheaval, imminent resolution seems unlikely. Nevertheless, history also suggests that in a time of crisis retrograde cultural manifestations such as the historicism of the 1970s and 1980s are, like the Black Death style, more expiatory than salutary, and fleeting at best. Similarly, as revelatory as the analysis and manifestations of post-structuralist philosophical speculation have been in recent years, only future developments will reveal whether they portend a fundamental change in society or are merely symptomatic productions of a culture conditioned, if not consumed, by successive crises.

Perhaps the least expected development in contemporary architecture is the emergence of a vibrant generation of architects working within the modernist tradition. Ironically, the key to understanding the vitality of this contemporary architecture is the now historic *dis*continuity of the modernist movement on both sides of the Atlantic. The critical architectural milieu created in part by the 1966 publication of Robert Venturi's *Complexity and Contradiction in Modern Architecture* contributed significantly to this breach. The work of the New York Five (Peter Eisenman, Michael Graves, Charles Gwathmey, John Hedjuk and Richard Meier) and of English architect James Stirling are emblematic of a self-conscious effort to create a gap between the postwar International Style and their own production during the 1970s. Existing on the periphery of professional practice, these architects often spent as much time writing and teaching as designing buildings. That their current works have evolved from a common investigation of the abstract language of prewar modernism to a formal heterogeneity reflects their experience as both participants in and critics of the postwar modern movement.

This discontinuity deepened with the arrival in the 1980s of a generation of architects conditioned by the broad cultural critiques of the late 1960s. This second wave of European modernists, represented by such figures as Zaha Hadid, Rem Koolhaas, Daniel Libeskind, Jean Nouvel, Bernard Tschumi and Peter Wilson, makes few direct references to the depredations of the latter-day International Style, which, ironically, had taken on the same meanings in Europe as it had in the United States. Their protracted formative periods, influenced by various relationships with the Institute for Architecture and Urban Studies in New York and the Architectural Association in London and with such figures as Alvin Boyarsky, Peter Eisenman and Kenneth Frampton, gave rise to an architectural production that, to use Hitchcock's phrase, is "at once new and intense."

The ease with which this second wave of architects integrates the legacies of pre- and postwar modernism is particularly evident in their unself-conscious attitudes toward the construction of an international architectural culture. It seems appropriate in this context to cite again Mumford's 1932 letter to Wright:

> No one can be merely an American, any more than [they] can be merely a New Yorker: we shall be at each other's throats, and have neither civilization or culture left, unless we become increasingly conscious of our common tasks and our common interests: this for architecture as well as anything else.

This generation of architects, encouraged by the growing political and economic unity of Western Europe, has had little if any regard for nationality. Tschumi's career and work provides a model: the designer was born in

100

Switzerland, educated in England, and is now based in New York with a practice in Paris. Paradoxically, Japan's astounding architectural production results from a national policy based on internationalism.

Western Europe's cultural and political fusion is, ironically, bracketed to the east by the recently re-nationalized states of *Mittel Europa* and the former Soviet Union and to the west by England, following a path of insular resistance to the European Community's *denouement*. England's continued emphasis on national character and its geographic determinism have resonated with particular strength in the United States in the last decade, revitalizing the Anglo-American cultural axis with distinct effects on architectural production. This common ground has proven fertile for the expansion of historicist manifestations of post-modernism. Paradoxically, Anglo-American aspirations for a national architecture seem to have risen in inverse proportion to the diminution of the relevance of national boundaries to contemporary economic and political realities. The effects flow in both directions: A group of American designers acts as semi-official purveyors of architecture to HRH the Prince of Wales, with Robert Venturi and Denise Scott Brown designing the Sainsbury Wing for London's National Gallery, while Ralph Lauren recycles the detritus of the Empire throughout its former colonies, resulting in an ill conceived coast-to-coast grafting of Colonial Williamsburg onto Wright's Broadacre City.

While Lauren's appeal to the tastes of the middle class has been achieved through the impressionistic tools of marketing, some of the rhetoric of the historicist debate has also entered the public consciousness. For a great many Americans modernism is effectively associated with "International Style slabs in their empty plazas" —the Willie Horton of architecture—despite the fact that the real estate industry has over the past decade levelled the playing field considerably with a great number of monstrous post-modern towers whose granite veneers and classical adornments do little to mitigate their overarching bulk and commodity orientation. Whether the public will eventually become disenchanted with historicist post-modernism is uncertain, but it is clear that, even in these conservative times, the public's consciousness of the architectural debate has rarely translated into ideological support. Despite the anti-modernism inherent in the post-modern program, the general public has not withheld its affection from modernist buildings in general, particularly those with a technological or cultural ethos such as the World Trade Towers in New York, the Vietnam War Memorial in Washington, D.C., the St. Louis Arch and the United Nations complex.

Nevertheless, American architects who describe themselves as modernists do so at considerable professional peril. Zaha Hadid and her colleagues in Europe have built relatively little to date, but current developments would suggest that they will soon have the opportunity to do so, while their generational counterparts in America, it seems, may not. Architects such as Steven Holl, Smith-Miller/Hawkinson, Morphosis (Michael Rotondi and Thom Mayne), Albert Pope and Tod Williams & Billy Tsien, despite nearly two decades of exemplary practices, continue to be overlooked for architectural commissions of any consequence in the United States. Their work can be considered a response, and necessarily a defensive one, to the architectural culture at large. While generally receptive to the more radical aspects of early modernism, most of their production is characterized by the ideological investigations possible in small projects: material theory and constructive process. The result has been a Scarpa-esque body of work wherein the physical aspects of the projects are imbued with critical positions far beyond their modest scale. Holl's recent housing project in Fukuoka, Japan, indicates that the broader implications of modernism can survive the compressive realities of contemporary practice in the United States. Nevertheless, the current obsession with simulation (historical, material and otherwise) suggests that the work of Holl and his American colleagues will continue to be marginalized at home.

Opposition to an ersatz national architectural agenda is not limited to this mid-career generation of designers, nor does it preclude the development of genuine local or regional schools of thought. Southern California and the Ticino district of Switzerland stand out as examples of vibrant architectural communities that belie the view that no collective production is possible. In this regard it is ironic to reintroduce Mumford as a latter day champion of the Bay Area school of architects after his disaffection with internationalist ideals. It may be that the future of architectural production rests simultaneously within and without the two positions.

SECTION ONE: MODERN ARCHITECTS

**Modern Architecture—
International Exhibition**

**The Museum of Modern Art
New York 10 February—
23 March 1932**

The initial proposal for an architectural exhibition submitted to the museum in December 1930 focused on the presentation of architectural models by nine "of the most prominent architects in the world." The proposal listed five Americans and four Europeans: Frank Lloyd Wright, Raymond Hood, Howe & Lescaze, Norman Bel Geddes, the Bowman Brothers, Le Corbusier, Mies van der Rohe, J.J.P. Oud and Walter Gropius. (Richard Neutra was eventually added and Bel Geddes dropped.) In this first conception the models were to represent different building types—a theater, a country house, a skyscraper, a prison as well as unbuilt works.

In time the *Modern Architects* section was expanded to include photographs of buildings completed by the various architects. The curators' attitudes toward the models evolved as well: in the final presentation the American models represented unbuilt works and the European models completed buildings. The survey of different building types became more limited and was, ultimately, heavily skewed toward single-family house's and school projects, both of which were considered to be accessible by the general public.

While the curators continued to refer to Exhibition 15 as an exhibition of architectural models, there were forty-eight photographs in Section One, a number of which were up to five feet long. Most of the projects were also represented in plans. This was many Americans' first view of such seminal works as Le Corbusier's Villa Savoye, Mies's Barcelona Pavilion and Gropius's Bauhaus. Wright's House on the Mesa, now relatively unknown, represented the high point of his interest in the European architectural developments of the 1920s.

The photographs reproduced here were taken from a large archive at the Museum of Modern Art that contains negatives of many of the photographs collected by Hitchcock and Johnson in preparing their book The International Style. *These photographs, with few exceptions, have been verified by installation photographs and/or other documents. The exterior view of the Villa Savoye that appeared in Exhibition 15 seems to have been lost. The existing archival image, reproduced here, appears to have been taken at the same time by the same photographer but from a different angle. The photo of Hood's Daily News Building reproduced here is one of two very similar images in the MoMA archives; the exhibition photograph cannot be distinguished in the installation photos. Some of the plan reproductions in the exhibition were taken from various publications although many (such as the Tugendhat House) were redrawn for Exhibition 15. In the instances where a plan image was missing from the MoMA archives an alternate was reproduced from contemporary publications. The title captions are taken from original documents.*

Mies van der Rohe

TUGENDHAT HOUSE, Brno, Czechoslovakia, 1930. Garden façade

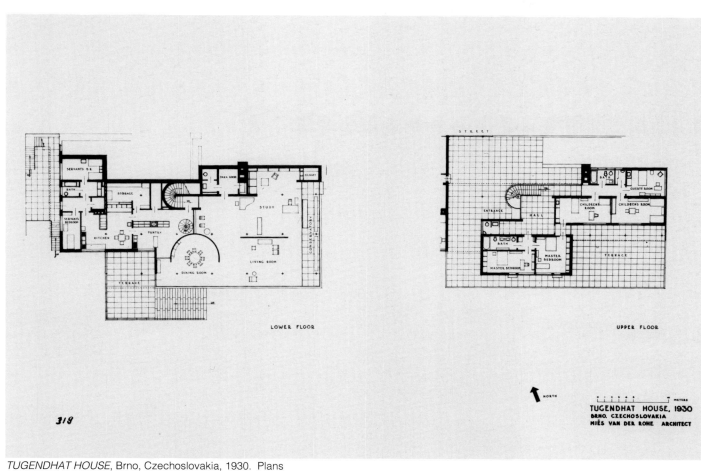

TUGENDHAT HOUSE, Brno, Czechoslovakia, 1930. Plans

TUGENDHAT HOUSE, Brno, Czechoslovakia, 1930. Interior view

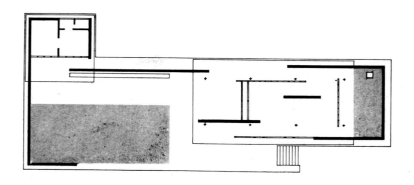

GERMAN PAVILION AT THE INTERNATIONAL EXPOSITION, Barcelona, Spain, 1929. Plan

GERMAN PAVILION AT THE INTERNATIONAL EXPOSITION, Barcelona, Spain, 1929. Interior view looking through to Kolbe statue

LANGE HOUSE, Krefeld, Germany, 1928.

APARTMENT INTERIOR, New York City, 1930.

Le Corbusier

SAVOYE HOUSE, Poissy-sur-Seine, France, 1930. Model

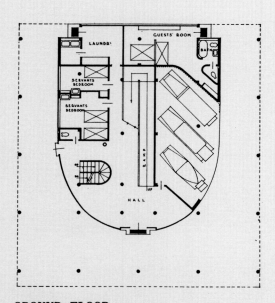

GROUND FLOOR

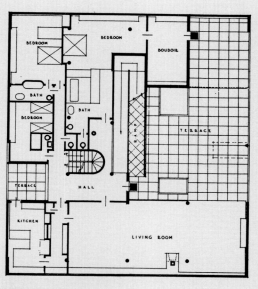

SECOND FLOOR

SAVOYE HOUSE, Poissy-sur-Seine, France, 1930. Plans

113

SAVOYE HOUSE, Poissy-sur-Seine, France, 1930. View from the north

SAVOYE HOUSE, Poissy-sur-Seine, France, 1930. Interior view

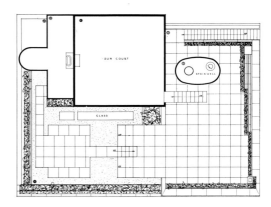

DE BEISTEGUI PENTHOUSE ROOF TERRACE, Paris, France, 1931. Plan

DE BEISTEGUI PENTHOUSE ROOF TERRACE, Paris, France, 1931.

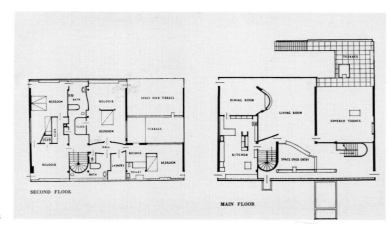

STEIN HOUSE (LES TERRASSES), Garches, France, 1928. Plans

STEIN HOUSE (LES TERRASSES), Garches, France, 1928. Garden façade

117

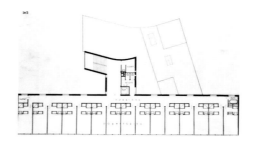

SWISS DORMITORY, CITÉ UNIVERSITAIRE, Paris, France, 1932. Plans

SWISS DORMITORY, CITÉ UNIVERSITAIRE, Paris, France, 1932. Perspectives

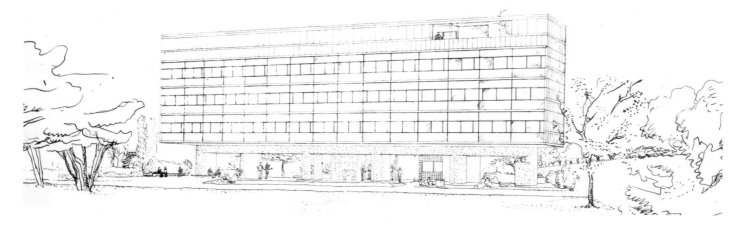

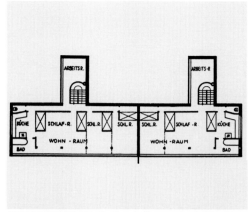

DOUBLE HOUSE, Stuttgart, Germany, 1927. Plan

DOUBLE HOUSE, Stuttgart, Germany, 1927. View from street

J. J. P. Oud

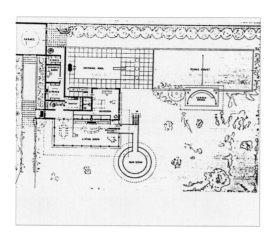

JOHNSON HOUSE, Pinehurst, North Carolina, 1931. Plan

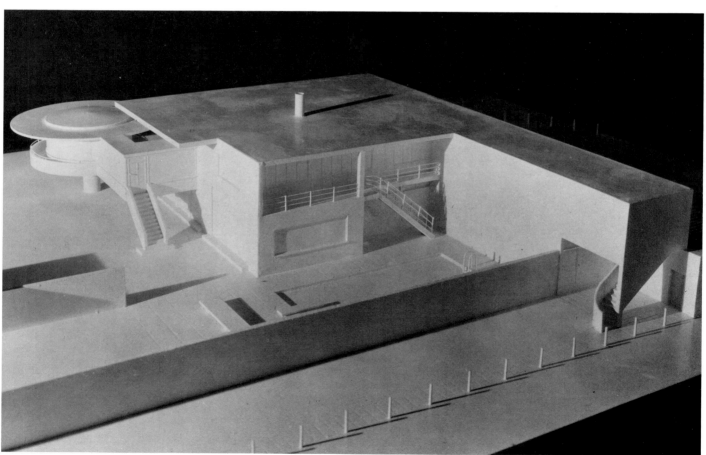

JOHNSON HOUSE, Pinehurst, North Carolina, 1931. Model

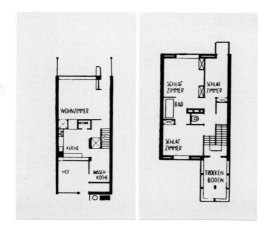

ROW OF SMALL HOUSES, Stuttgart, Germany, 1927. Plans

ROW OF SMALL HOUSES, Stuttgart, Germany, 1927.

121

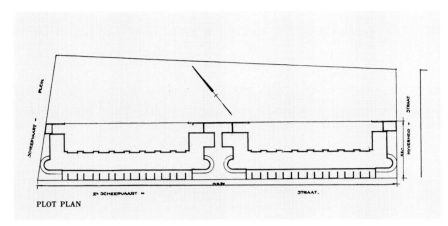

PLOT PLAN

SHOP FRONT, Hook of Holland, 1927. Site Plan

SHOP FRONT, Hook of Holland, 1927.

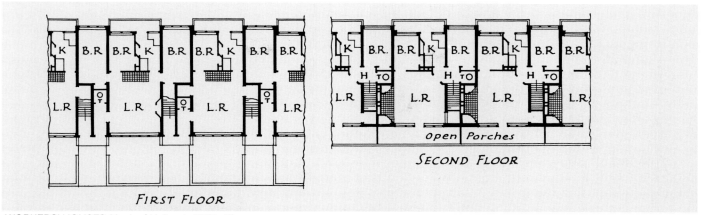

FIRST FLOOR   SECOND FLOOR

WORKERS' HOUSES, Hook of Holland, 1927. Plan

WORKERS' HOUSES, Hook of Holland, 1927.

123

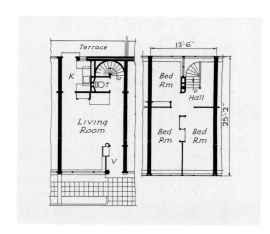

SHOPS KIEFHOEK DEVELOPMENT, Rotterdam, Netherlands, 1930. Plan

SHOPS KIEFHOEK DEVELOPMENT, Rotterdam, Netherlands, 1930.

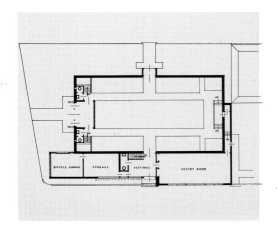

CHURCH, KIEFHOEK DEVELOPMENT, Rotterdam, Netherlands, 1930. Plan

CHURCH, KIEFHOEK DEVELOPMENT, Rotterdam, Netherlands, 1930.

Frank Lloyd Wright

PROJECT FOR A HOUSE ON THE MESA, Denver, Colorado, 1932. Model

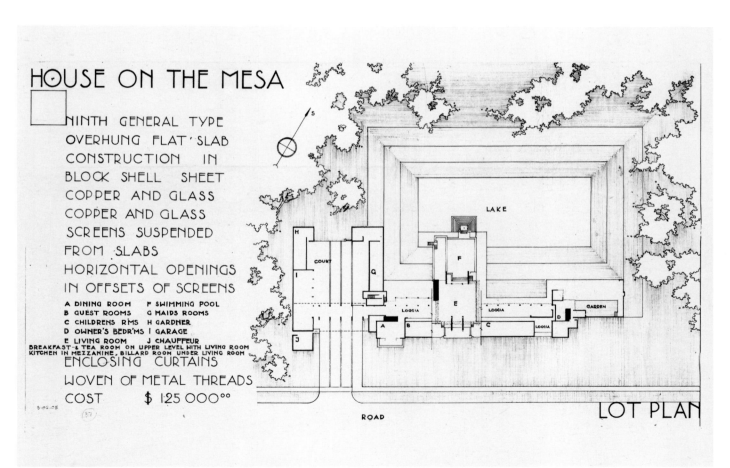

HOUSE ON THE MESA

NINTH GENERAL TYPE
OVERHUNG FLAT SLAB
CONSTRUCTION IN
BLOCK SHELL SHEET
COPPER AND GLASS
COPPER AND GLASS
SCREENS SUSPENDED
FROM SLABS
HORIZONTAL OPENINGS
IN OFFSETS OF SCREENS

A DINING ROOM   F SWIMMING POOL
B GUEST ROOMS   G MAIDS ROOMS
C CHILDRENS RMS H GARDNER
D OWNER'S BEDR'MS I GARAGE
E LIVING ROOM   J CHAUFFEUR
BREAKFAST-& TEA ROOM ON UPPER LEVEL WITH LIVING ROOM
KITCHEN IN MEZZANINE, BILLARD ROOM UNDER LIVING ROOM

ENCLOSING CURTAINS
WOVEN OF METAL THREADS
COST $ 125 000°°

LAKE

COURT

LOT PLAN

ROAD

LOGGIA   GARDEN

PROJECT FOR A HOUSE ON THE MESA, Denver, Colorado, 1932.
Plan and prospectus.

127

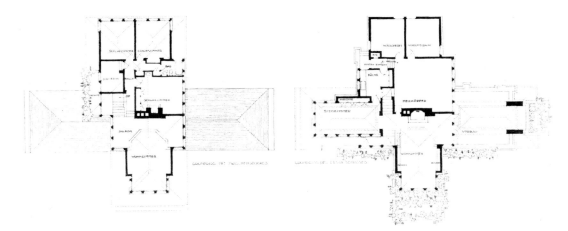

ROBERTS HOUSE, River
Forest, Illinois, 1907. Plan

ROBERTS HOUSE, River Forest, Illinois, 1907.

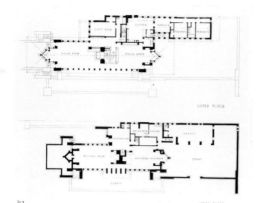

ROBIE HOUSE, Chicago, Illinois, 1909. Plans

ROBIE HOUSE, Chicago, Illinois, 1909. Exterior view

129

TALIESIN, Spring Green, Wisconsin, 1925.

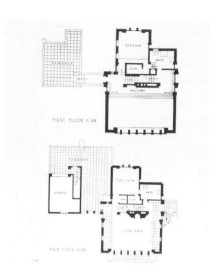

MILLARD HOUSE, Pasadena,
California, 1921. Plan

MILLARD HOUSE, Pasadena, California, 1921. Exterior view

131

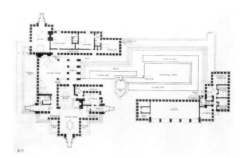

JONES HOUSE, Tulsa, Oklahoma, 1931. Plan

JONES HOUSE, Tulsa, Oklahoma, 1931. Partial exterior view

JONES HOUSE, Tulsa, Oklahoma, 1931. Aerial view

133

Howe & Lescaze

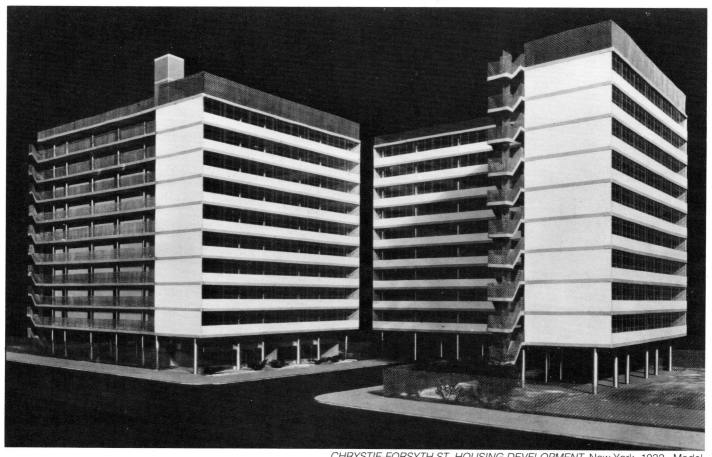

CHRYSTIE-FORSYTH ST. HOUSING DEVELOPMENT, New York, 1932. Model

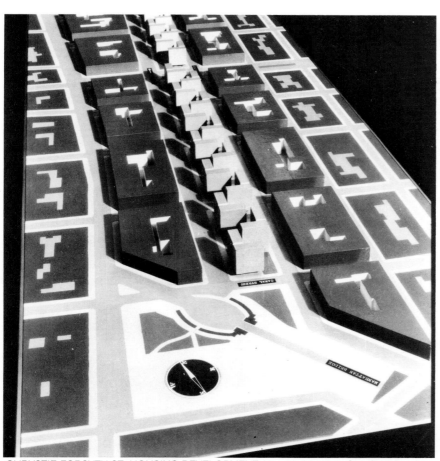

CHRYSTIE-FORSYTH ST. HOUSING DEVELOPMENT, New York, 1932. Site model

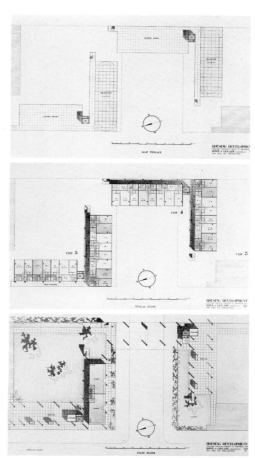

CHRYSTIE-FORSYTH ST. HOUSING DEVELOPMENT, New York, 1932. Plans

135

TRANSLUX THEATRE, New York City, 1931.

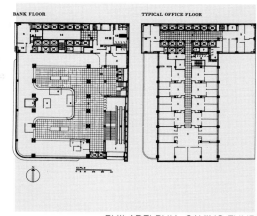

PHILADELPHIA SAVING FUND SOCIETY BUILDING, Philadelphia, Pennsylvania, 1932. Plans

PHILADELPHIA SAVING FUND SOCIETY BUILDING, Philadelphia, Pennsylvania, 1932.

137

F. V. Storrs, 1932.   Interior

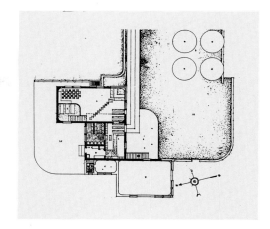

OAK LANE COUNTRY DAY SCHOOL, Philadelphia, Pennsylvania, 1929. Plan

OAK LANE COUNTRY DAY SCHOOL, Philadelphia, Pennsylvania, 1929.

139

HESSIAN HILLS SCHOOL, Croton-on-Hudson, New York, 1931.

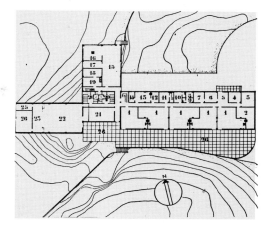

HESSIAN HILLS SCHOOL, Croton-on-Hudson, New York, 1931. Plan

HESSIAN HILLS SCHOOL, Croton-on-Hudson, New York, 1931. Interior view

Walter Gropius

BAUHAUS, Dessau, Germany, 1926. Model

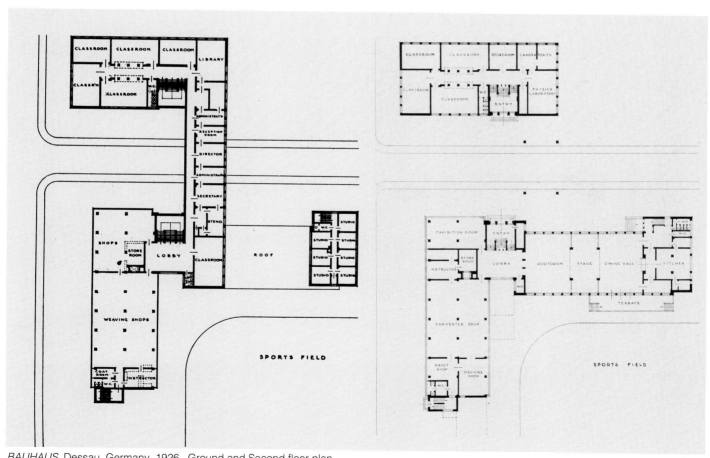

BAUHAUS, Dessau, Germany, 1926. Ground and Second floor plan

BAUHAUS, Dessau, Germany, 1926. Workshop wing

BAUHAUS, Dessau, Germany, 1927. Living quarters, administration, etc.

BAUHAUS, DIRECTOR'S HOUSE, Dessau, Germany, 1926. Plan

BAUHAUS, DIRECTOR'S HOUSE, Bauhaus, Dessau, Germany, 1926.

FAGUS FACTORY, Alfeld, Germany, 1914.

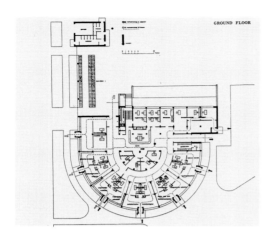

GROUND FLOOR

CITY EMPLOYMENT OFFICE, Dessau, Germany, 1928. Plan

CITY EMPLOYMENT OFFICE, Dessau, Germany, 1928.

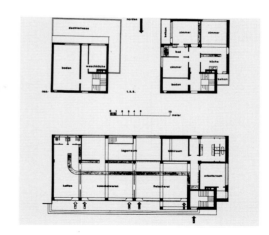

COOPERATIVE STORE AND APARTMENTS, Dessau, Germany, 1928. Plans

COOPERATIVE STORE AND APARTMENTS, Dessau, Germany, 1928.

Bowman Brothers

PROJECT FOR THE LUX APARTMENTS, Evanston, Illinois, 1931. Model

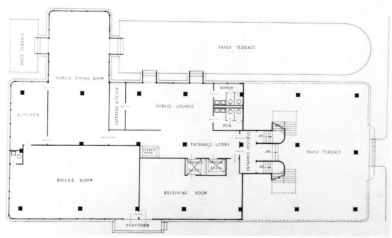

PROJECT FOR LUX APARTMENTS, Evanston, Illinois, 1931. Plans.

151

PROJECT FOR BUSINESS BLOCK, 1931.

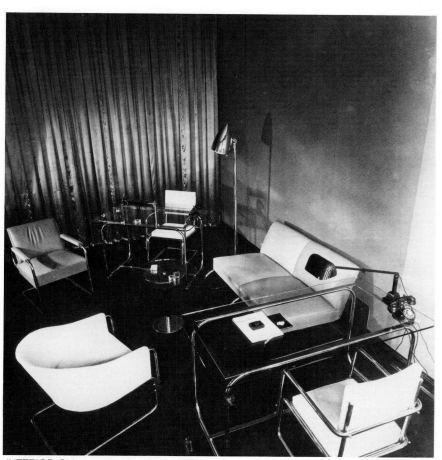

INTERIOR, Chicago, Illinois, 1930.

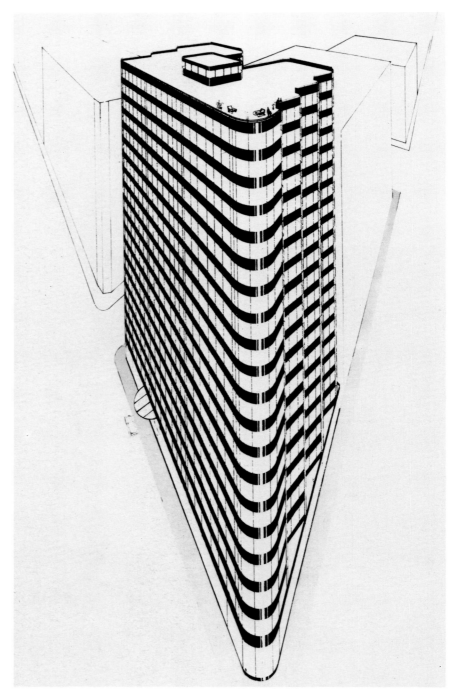

PROJECT FOR APARTMENT HOUSE, 1931.

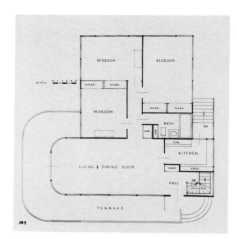

PROJECT FOR A PREFABRICATED HOUSE, 1930. Plan

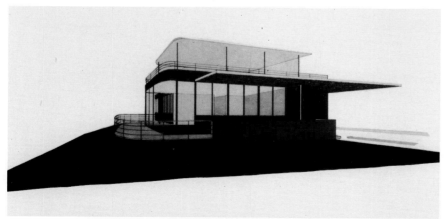

PROJECT FOR A PREFABRICATED HOUSE, 1930. Two perspectives

155

Richard Neutra

PROJECT FOR RING PLAN SCHOOL, "Rush City Reformed", 1928-1931. Model

156

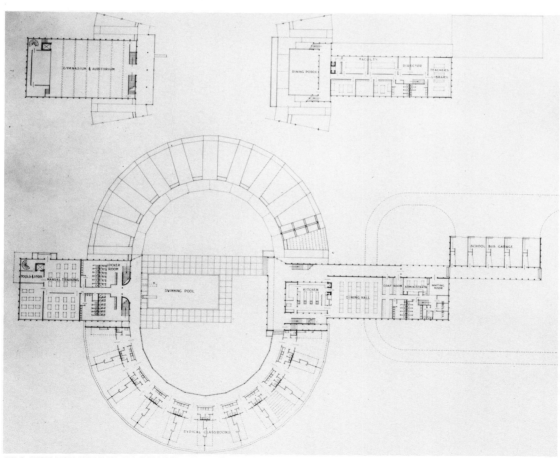

PROJECT FOR RING PLAN SCHOOL, "Rush City Reformed", 1928-1931. Plan.

PROJECT FOR A SKYSCRAPER, 1927.

JARDINETTE APARTMENTS, Los Angeles, California, 1927. Exterior view

LOVELL HOUSE, Los Angeles, California, 1929. Exterior view

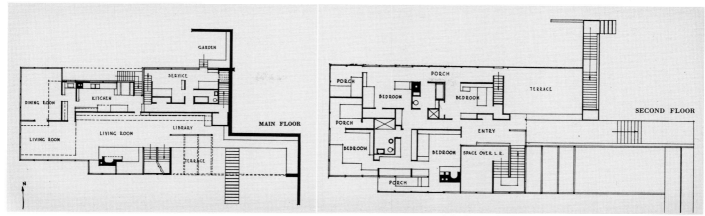

LOVELL HOUSE, Los Angeles, California, 1929. Plans

LOVELL HOUSE, Los Angeles, California, 1929. Interior view

Raymond Hood

PROJECT FOR AN APARTMENT TOWER IN THE COUNTRY, 1932. Model

PROJECT FOR AN APARTMENT TOWER IN THE COUNTRY, 1932. Plot plan showing land divided into typical suburban lots

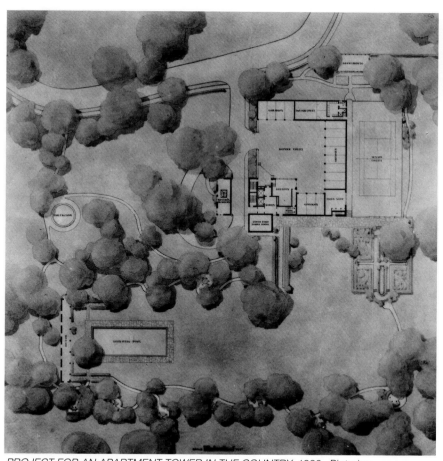

PROJECT FOR AN APARTMENT TOWER IN THE COUNTRY, 1932. Plot plan

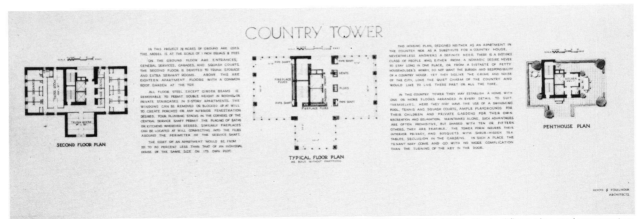

PROJECT FOR AN APARTMENT TOWER IN THE COUNTRY, 1932. Typical floor plan and prospectus

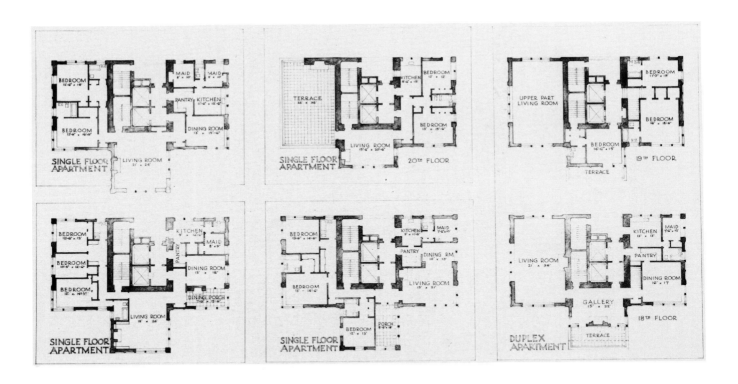

PROJECT FOR AN APARTMENT TOWER IN THE COUNTRY, 1932. Typical floor plans

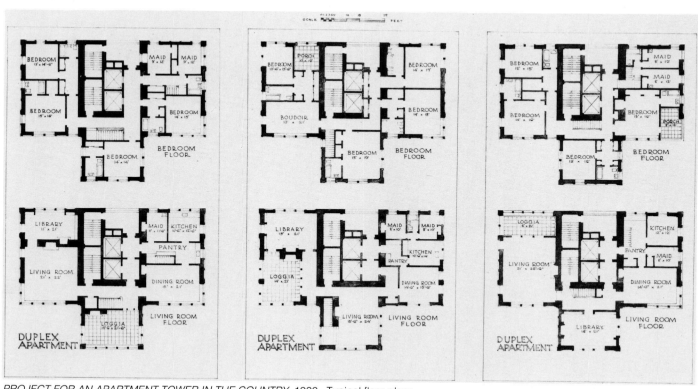

PROJECT FOR AN APARTMENT TOWER IN THE COUNTRY, 1932. Typical floor plans

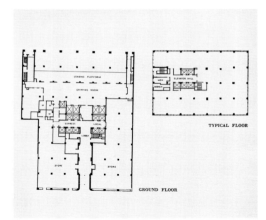

(with André Fouilhoux) *McGRAW-HILL BUILDING*, New York City, 1931. Plans

(with André Fouilhoux) *McGRAW-HILL BUILDING*, New York City, 1931.

166

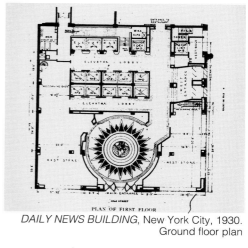

DAILY NEWS BUILDING, New York City, 1930.
Ground floor plan

DAILY NEWS BUILDING, New York City, 1930.

AMERICAN RADIATOR BUILDING,
New York City, 1924.

AMERICAN RADIATOR BUILDING, New York City, 1924. Plans

168

PATTERSON HOUSE, Ossining, New York, 1930.

SECTION TWO: THE EXTENT OF MODERN ARCHITECTURE

As opposed to Section One, which focused on the works of individual architects, Section Two was organized by country to demonstrate the global character of "the style."

In the first proposal accepted by the museum, one section of the exhibition was to be devoted to the winning entries of an international competition for young architects. While this component was soon dropped, the Extent of Modern Architecture section was not added until late in the planning process. Like the international competition proposal, it provided a global rather than strictly Euro-American perspective.

The Extent section included forty projects by thirty-seven architects from fifteen countries. Each project was represented by a single photograph not accompanied by plans or drawings. Most of the photographs were drawn from those collected by Hitchcock and Johnson in preparing their book. Most of the architects exhibited a single project; Andre Lurçat, Eric Mendelsohn and Nicolaiev & Firsenko were represented by two projects each. Ernst May and Otto Haesler both had projects in the Extent as well as in the Housing section.

The photographs presented here, with few exceptions, were reproduced from MoMA's archival negatives and verified by various documents. The photograph of Rob Mallet-Stevens's Villa at Hyeres was selected arbitrarily from four views of the villa in the MoMA archives. The view of the Starret-Lehigh industrial building was also selected from several images. The negative of Howell & Tucker's laboratory is missing from the MoMA archives and the photograph of the laboratory used in The International Style, *which may or may not be the same, is reproduced here. There are two identical negatives of Clauss & Daub's filling station in the MoMA archives, although one has been altered to remove an apparently offending Victorian house. The altered image has been reproduced here, the unaltered image is reproduced on page 80.*

170

BELGIUM

H. L. de Konick, Lenglet House, near Brussels, 1926

AUSTRIA

Lois Welzenbacher, *APARTMENT HOUSE*, Innsbruck, 1930.

NETHERLANDS

W. J. Duiker, *OPEN AIR SCHOOL*, Amsterdam, 1931.

NETHERLANDS

G. Rietveld, *HOUSE AT UTRECHT*, 1924.

Brinkman & van der Lugt, *VAN NELLE TOBACCO,
TEA & COFFEE FACTORY*, Rotterdam, 1930.

Thompson & Churchill, *OFFICE BUILDING*,
New York City, 1931.

173

U.S.A.

Frederic Kiesler, *FILM GUILD CINEMA*, New York City. As executed

U.S.A.

Frederic Kiesler, *FILM GUILD CINEMA*, New York City. As designed

174

R.G. & W.M. Cory, *STARRETT-LEHIGH BUILDING*, New York City, 1931.

Tucker & Howell, *HIGHLANDS MUSEUM AND BIOLOGICAL LABORATORY*,
Highlands, North Carolina, 1931.

U.S.A.

Kocher & Frey, *HARRISON HOUSE*, Long Island,
New York, 1931.

U.S.A.

Clauss & Daub, *FILLING STATION FOR THE STANDARD
OIL CO. OF OHIO*, Cleveland, 1931.

SWITZERLAND

Artaria & Schmidt, *RESIDENCE FOR PROFESSIONAL WOMEN*, Basel, 1930.

SWITZERLAND

Max Ernst Haefeli, *APARTMENT HOUSE*, Zurich, 1929.

SWITZERLAND

Carl Weidemeyer, *HOUSE ON LAGO MAGGIORE*, 1929.

SPAIN

Labayen & Aizpurna, *CLUBHOUSE*, San Sebastian, 1930.

Paul Nelson, *PHARMACY*, Paris, 1931.

Rob Mallet-Stevens, *DE NOAILLES VILLA*, Hyéres, 1925.

FRANCE

André Lurçat, *FRORIEP DE SALIS HOUSE*, France, 1927.

FRANCE

Gabriel Guevrekian, *VILLA HEIM*, Neuilly-sur-Seine, France, 1928.

FRANCE

André Lurçat, *HOTEL NORD-SUD*, Calvi, Corsica, 1931.

GERMANY

Otto Haesler, *OLD PEOPLE'S HOME*, Kassel, 1931.

GERMANY

Erich Mendelsohn, *HOUSE OF THE ARCHITECT*, Berlin, 1930.

GERMANY

Erich Mendelsohn, *SCHOCKEN DEPARTMENT STORE*, Chemnitz, 1930.

Office of the City Architect-Ernst May, *FRIEDERICH EBERT SCHOOL*, Frankfort-on-Main, 1931.

Luckhardt & Anker, *ROW OF HOUSES,* Berlin, 1930.

GERMANY

Hans Scharoun, *WOHNHEIM,* Breslau, 1930.

GERMANY

Karl Schneider, *KUNSTVEREIN*, Hamburg, 1930.

Eskil Sundahl, *SEIDLUNG OF THE SWEDISH COOPERATIVE SOCIETY,*
near Stockholm, 1930.

Markelius & Ahren, *STUDENT'S CLUBHOUSE,* Stockholm, 1930.

ENGLAND

Amyas Connell, *HOUSE IN AMSERSHAM*, Buckinghamshire, 1931.

ENGLAND

Joseph Emberton, *ROYAL CORINTHIAN YACHT CLUB*, Burnham-on-Crouch, 1931.

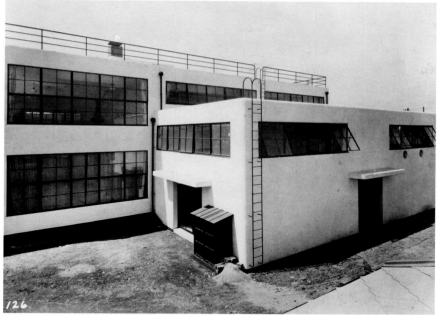

Mamoru Yamada, *ELECTRICAL LABORATORY*, Tokyo, 1930.

Isaburo Ueno, *STAR BAR*, Kyoto, 1931.

USSR

Nicolaiev & Fissenko, *ELECTRO-PHYSICAL LABORATORY*, Moscow, 1927.

USSR

Nicolaiev & Fissenko, *ELECTRO-TECHNICAL INSTITUTE*, Moscow, 1927.

Ludvik Kysela, *BATA STORE*, Prague, 1929.

Otto Eisler, *HOUSE FOR TWO BROTHERS*, Brno, 1931.

CZECHOSLOVAKIA

Bohuslav Fuchs, *STUDENT'S CLUBHOUSE*, Brno, 1931.

FINLAND

Alvar Aalto, *TURUN SANOMAT BUILDING*, Turku, 1930.

L. Figini & G. Pollini, *ELECTRICAL HOUSE AT THE MONZA EXHIBITION*, 1930.

SECTION THREE: HOUSING

Clarence Stein and Henry Wright,
Radburn, N.J., 1928.

Springsteen & Hammer, Amalgamated Grand
Street Apartments, N.Y.C., 1929-37.

The third section of Exhibition 15 focused on housing, the last remaining element of a more ambitious Industrial section that was to present exhibitions on large-scale urban construction, a technologically advanced factory prototype and an "industrial housing project."

Soon after the proposal for an architectural exhibition was approved by the museum Johnson asked Lewis Mumford to curate the Housing section. While there is little evidence of Mumford's personal involvement, his colleagues (Catherine Bauer, Henry Wright and Clarence Stein) provided Johnson with drawings and photos of American housing projects as well as didactic text panels that reflected Mumford's thinking at the time. Johnson provided photographs of European housing projects and arranged the loan of Otto Haesler's model of the Rothenberg *Siedlung* in Kassel, Germany, which became the focus of the Housing section.

Many of the photographs in Section Three were placed to either side of the text panels for illustrative purposes (see page 78). Evident in the installation photographs are texts entitled "Slum Improvement" (comparing European and American housing projects), "Block Development" (comparing the court of Stein & Wright's Sunnyside Gardens with a jumble of typical lot-line rear yards) and "Slum-Superslum" (which points out the similar densities of both the "luxurious" Upper East Side and the tenements of the Lower East Side). Another "triptych," partially off camera, illustrated Stein & Wright's housing project at Radburn, N.J.

Some of the photographs and all of the text panels evident in the installation photographs no longer exist in the museum's archives. Several photographs are listed in various documents but cannot be verified by the installation photographs. The plan of Radburn on this page appears in the catalogue but cannot be verified elsewhere. The photograph of the Amalgamated Grand Street Apartments on this page is taken from a contemporary journal as is the text "Slum Improvement" (opposite) that appears in a special issue of Shelter magazine *devoted to Exhibition 15 and seems to have been taken from the Housing section. (see p.79) All other material is taken from the exhibition catalogue and MoMA archives.*

SLUM IMPROVEMENT

NEW YORK CITY
231 Families
Apartments built with the aid of subsidy in the form of tax-exemption.
Because of exorbitant land-costs, too expensive for lower income groups.
No playgrounds except small recreation space on roof.
No private gardens.
60% coverage of land by 6-story building.
Rooms face:
      Noisy traffic street, or
Narrow dark street, or Interior Court.
Philanthropic private investment with limited return.
Isolated; not part of a larger plan.
Land values, inflated because of unfounded expectation of skyscrapers, necessitate tall apartment buildings.

ROTTERDAM
300 Families
Houses for large families, built by the city.
Because land was city-owned, inexpensive enough for lower income groups.
2 large playgrounds.
A private garden for each family.
50% coverage of land by 2-story buildings. (3 times as much sun.)
Rooms face:
      Quiet local traffic streets,
      or
      Private sunny gardens.
Municipal investment.
Part of wide plan for slum-rehabilitation.
Single family house possible because of normal land-value. No anticipation of congestion.

Conclusion: REHABILITATION OF SLUMS IS POSSIBLE.

BUT THE PRESENT POPULATION OF THE SLUMS CANNOT BE REHOUSED WITHOUT DRASTIC CHANGES IN FINANCE POLICY AND WITHOUT SCALING DOWN INFLATED LAND VALUES.

Text panel (as published in *Shelter*, April 1932).

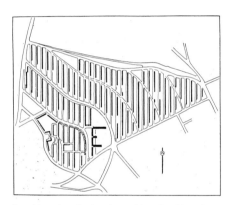

Otto Haesler, Rothenberg Housing Development,
Kassel, 1930-32. Site Plan

Otto Haesler, Rothenberg Housing Development, Kassel, 1930- 32. Model

Otto Haesler, Rothenberg Housing Development, Kassel, 1930-32. Street view

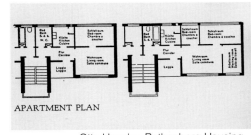

APARTMENT PLAN

Otto Haesler, Rothenberg Housing
Development, Kassel, 1930-32. Typical unit

Otto Haesler, Rothenberg Housing Development, Kassel, 1930-32. Aerial view

Ernst May & Associates, Römerstadt Housing Development, Frankfurt-am-Main,
1927-28. Aerial view

Typical Block of Row Houses in Long Island City, N.Y. View of lot line court

Clarence Stein & Henry Wright, Sunnyside Gardens, Long Island, N.Y., 1924-28.
View of interior garden

J.J.P. Oud, Kiefhoek Housing Development, 1928-30. Aerial view

Introduction

1. While frequently referred to as the "International Style Exhibition," both the exhibition and catalogue shared the same name: Modern Architecture—International Exhibition. (Catalogue by Henry-Russell Hitchcock, Philip Johnson and Lewis Mumford [New York: Museum of Modern Art, 1932]). Also published as *Modern Architects* (New York: Museum of Modern Art and W. W. Norton, 1932). The discrepancy between the two titles is due to an arrangement between the publisher and the museum: "Some of the books produced by the Museum and bound in paper cover for sale at the Museum were selected by the firm for publication, hard bound in cloth and sold through the bookstores" (from a typescript entitled "An Account of the Early Days of W. W. Norton and Co.," by Howard P. Wilson, W. W. Norton Editorial Archives, Columbia University). *Modern Architects* was the title of the trade version of the catalogue.

2. Philip Johnson, "Memorandum on the Architectural Exhibition," 24 September 1931, Museum Archives, MoMA, N.Y.

3. Henry–Russell Hitchcock and Philip Johnson, *The International Style: Architecture Since 1922* (New York: W. W. Norton, 1932; reprint, 1966).

4. Much of the current literature on Exhibition 15 is thus dependent on the catalogue. For the historical record I have tried to cite throughout this essay recently published errors of fact. These errors should not be considered as evidence of poor scholarship or as discrediting the works as many of the original sources cited in this essay were previously unavailable for research.

For example, Arthur Drexler and Thomas S. Hines relied on the catalogue in researching their book *The Architecture of Richard Neutra* (New York: Museum of Modern Art, 1982). Therein they list Neutra's Zehlendorf houses as having been exhibited (they weren't) and omit Neutra's skyscraper design for his Rush City Reformed proposals, which was in the exhibition.

Franz Schulze's *Mies van der Rohe: A Critical Biography* (Chicago: University of Chicago Press, 1985) lists the Barcelona Pavilion, Tugendhat House and Lange House (83) as having been exhibited but omits the Johnson apartment.

Similarly, in Robert Stern, Gregory Gilmartin and Thomas Mellin's *New York 1930: Architecture and Urbanism Between the Two World Wars* (New York: Rizzoli, 1987) the authors note that the "show contained seventy–five photographs and ten models" (344). Research for this essay reveals the actual figures to be ninety-nine photographs (including six photographs of perspective drawings) and eleven models.

Lawrence Wodehouse's *The Roots of International Style Architecture* (West Cornwall, Conn.: Locust Hill Press, 1991) is also based on the catalogue, and his list of the works by Wright in the exhibition (note 1, p. 110) should be amended: the W. H. Winslow House, the 1894 project for an office building, the Ocatilla Camp and the Larkin Factory were not in Exhibition 15 (see below). Also, a photograph of a model for an all-metal structure published in the July 1930 issue of *Architectural Record* as a "Lake Front Building" is incorrectly labeled as the Lux Apartment project.

Suzanne Stephens's research on Exhibition 15 (*Skyline* [February 1982]: 20–23) extends beyond the catalogue and involves a preliminary review of the museum's archives. Her footnotes, however, indicate unresolved discrepancies between documents, specifically the museum's photo archives and a post–installation memo by Johnson. Research for this essay indicates that the memo is more accurate than the photo archives and that Stephens's index should be amended: Wright's Winslow House and Ocatilla Camp, Lescaze's House of the Architect, Slaato's Three Family House and El Lissitzky's Niedersachsische Landesgalerie were not in Exhibition 15, although a photograph of Wright's Ocatilla Camp was substituted for one of the images of the Jones House (see pp. 10 & 133 respectively) in the traveling exhibition. Also, the Bowman Brothers' Project for a House should read "Project for an Apartment House" and Hans Scharoun's Breslau School is actually entitled "Wohnheim, a Residence for Single Men."

5. This accelerated production schedule was not unusual for the museum's publications of the period.

6. For convenience, "curators" is used to collectively describe Barr, Hitchcock and Johnson even though it is more accurate to refer to them as the museum director, the exhibition's guest curator and the exhibition director, respectively. Similarly, the term "authors" refers to Hitchcock and Johnson, acknowledging their joint effort in producing the book. Nonetheless, all parties recognize that Hitchcock played the dominant role in constructing the intellectual arguments contained therein. As Barr put it in 1948: "It is not my formula at all but one arrived at by Hitchcock and Johnson, principally Hitchcock who, although he now seems evasive about it, was teacher and theorist for both Johnson and I" (Alfred H. Barr Jr. to Lewis Mumford, 27 February 1948, Mumford Papers, University of Pennsylvania). When appropriate I attempt to distinguish their individual roles.

7. Philip Johnson has provided Franz Schulze with personal correspondence from this period for Schulze's biography of Johnson in progress. Schulze and Johnson generously provided copies of the correspondence from 1930. These letters, and all other correspondence cited, are presented without editorial corrections unless noted otherwise.

8. For information on Barr's role in appointing Gropius to the faculty of the Harvard School of Architecture, see Margaret Scolari Barr, "Our Campaigns: 1930–1944," *New Criterion*, special issue (Summer 1987): 46.

Part One

1. Philip Johnson (the Hague) to Mrs. Homer H. (Louise Pope) Johnson, 20 June 1930, Philip Johnson Papers. Russell's "big book" is *Modern Architecture: Romanticism and Reintegration* (New York: Payson and Clarke, 1929; reprint New York: Hacker, 1970).

Endnotes - Part One (p. 12 to p. 18)

2. Before beginning work on *Modern Architecture* Hitchcock writes to Barr: "My appetite for the avant-garde will carry me through the book I hope then back to the past. I have really enjoyed making analyses of late Gothic and Baroque, etc." (Henry-Russell Hitchcock to Alfred H. Barr Jr., 12 August 1928, Museum Archives, MoMA, N.Y.) Similarly, after finishing his first book on modern architecture Hitchcock writes: "My own next labors will be on Romantic architecture as I call that from 1750–1850 with which I have already dealt a little in my *Modern Architecture* book. I trust we may find ourselves nearer in accord in the past and in the future than in the immediate present which with death of my friend Peter Smith in whom I had such hopes as coming American architect seems somewhat flat and stale for the time being" (Henry-Russell Hitchcock to Lewis Mumford, 21 June 1929, Lewis Mumford Papers, University of Pennsylvania).

3. Alfred H. Barr Jr., "Modern Architecture," *The Hound and Horn* 3, no. 3 (April–June 1930): 431–35.

4. Margaret Scolari Barr, "Philip Johnson," typescript of the early history of the museum, 12, Museum Archives, MoMA, N.Y.

5. Of the museum's circle of young aesthetes, Marga Barr writes: "Johnson was part of the group that assembled around Alfred for the art of the Now" (M. S. Barr, typescript, 12, Museum Archives, MoMA, N.Y.).

6. For this and other aspects of Hitchcock's background I have relied on Helen Searing's "Henry-Russell Hitchcock: The Architectural Historian as Critic and Connoisseur" in *The Architectural Historian in America,* E. B. MacDougall, gen. ed., *Studies in the History of Art* 35 (Washington, D.C.: National Gallery of Art, 1990), 251–63.

7. Johnson recalls meeting Hitchcock at Harvard during his final year of studies (1929–1930) while Margaret Barr claimed she introduced Johnson to Hitchcock at Vassar during the 1928–1929 school year. See Russell Lynes, *Good Old Modern* (New York: Atheneum, 1973), 84; and M. S. Barr, typescript, 17, Museum Archives, MoMA, N.Y.

8. Philip Johnson (Hamburg) to Mrs. Homer H. Johnson, 7 July 1930, Johnson Papers.

9. Gustav Platz, *Die Baukunst der neuesten Zeit* (Berlin: Propylaenverlag, 1927; reprint 1931). Among other titles this publication figures prominently in Hitchcock's bibliographies of the time: Platz's book is mentioned in *Modern Architecture* and *Modern Architecture— International Exhibition* and is included in Hitchcock's "Selected List of Books," *Architectural Record* 65 (March 1929): 175. Johnson also cites Platz in his first publication, a review of Cheney's *New World Architecture* ("Modernism in Architecture," *The New Republic,* 18 March 1931, 134).

10. Philip Johnson (Copenhagen) to Mrs. Homer H. Johnson, 4 July 1930, Johnson Papers. It should be noted that the "dirty work" to which Johnson refers is "to collect the photos from dilatory architects" (Johnson to Mrs. H. Johnson, 20 June 1930, Johnson Papers).

11. Johnson to Mrs. H. Johnson, 7 July 1930, Johnson Papers.

12. Philip Johnson (Berlin) to Mrs. Homer H. Johnson, 21 July (1930), Johnson Papers.

13. Otto Haesler to Johnson (Berlin), undated (October 1930) response to Johnson's (Berlin) letter of 30 September 1930, Museum Archives, MoMA, N.Y. For a discussion of the use of the term "International Style," see Notes, p. 89.

14. The terms "new traditionalist" and (awkwardly) "new pioneers" are used in Hitchcock's *Modern Architecture* to characterize, respectively, the prewar figures of Wright, Behrens, Perret and Van de Velde and the postwar figures of Le Corbusier, Gropius, Oud and, tentatively, Mies.

15. Hitchcock and Johnson, *The International Style*, 27.

16. Ibid., 24–27. In addition to "half-modern," the authors also frequently use the terms "modernistic" or "pseudo-modern" (usually with quotation marks) to denigrate work that doesn't conform to their conception of modernism.

They use the term broadly but most often in reference to work influenced by the 1925 Exposition des Arts Decoratifs: the art deco movement in America. Catherine Bauer adds yet another term to this critical lexicon: "modernique" (Catherine Bauer to Lewis Mumford, 6 February 1931, Mumford Papers, University of Pennsylvania).

17. Hitchcock, *Modern Architecture,* 162 [emphasis added].

18. Henry-Russell Hitchcock, "Four Harvard Architects," *The Hound and Horn* 2, no. 1 (September 1928): 41–47 [emphasis added].

19. Hitchcock and Johnson, *The International Style,* 29–33. In these pages the authors construct a rather difficult chronological artifice, in which they discern the simultaneous and near spontaneous generation of the International Style in 1922 as evidenced in Oud's Oud–Mathenese housing project, Le Corbusier's Citrohan house and Mies's brick country house. Aside from the numerous historical problems in viewing 1922 as a unique historic threshold, they were incorrect in saying that Mies's project was designed in 1922. It was designed in 1924.

20. "It is impossible to find any buildings truly reflecting a new aesthetic until 1922 when they appeared contemporaneously in France and Holland; and immediately afterward in Germany" (Hitchcock, *Modern Architecture,* 157). "The year 1922 was of great importance for contemporary architecture, for in it appeared also the first really and wholly new work of Le Corbusier and Gropius" (Henry-Russell Hitchcock, "The Architectural Work of J.J.P. Oud," *The Arts* [February 1928]: 102).

21. Barr, "Modern Architecture," 433.

22. Henry-Russell Hitchcock, "The Decline of Architecture," *The Hound and Horn* 1, no. 1 (September 1931): 28–35 (citation from 31).

23. Philip Johnson (Berlin) to Mrs. Homer H. Johnson, 6 August (1930), Johnson Papers.

Part Two

1. M. S. Barr, typescript, 15, Museum Archives, MoMA, N.Y.

2. "[Neuman] has made me if I want the American editor of *Die Form*, one of the best German modern magazines" (Johnson to Mrs. H. Johnson, 7 July 1930, Johnson Papers). Johnson first contacts the Bowman Brothers (Irving and Monroe) for an article for *Die Form* on their prefabricated house designs (Johnson to Bowman Brothers, 23 October 1930, Registrar's Archives, MoMA, N.Y.).

3. Philip Johnson, "Modernism in Architecture," *The New Republic,* (18 March 1931), 134. It appears that this brief article, which was the introduction to a longer piece, was written in late 1930 and sent to Mumford for comment (Johnson to Mumford, 3 January 1931, Mumford Papers, University of Pennsylvania).

4. See Notes pg. 89 for a detailed discussion of Exhibition 15's chronology.

5. In this essay, "exhibit" refers to a single element of the "exhibition"; the latter refers to the entire installation.

6. Johnson to Mumford, 3 January 1931, Mumford Papers, University of Pennsylvania.

7. *Historical Statistics of the United States—Colonial Times to 1970* (Washington, D.C.: U.S. Department of Commerce, 1976) Table G 319–336, "Family Personal Income."

8. Philip Johnson, "The Architectural Exhibition for the Museum of Modern Art in 1932," February 1931, Museum Archives, MoMA, N.Y.

9. Interview with Peter Eisenman, *Skyline* (February 1982): 14.

10. Hitchcock, *Modern Architecture,* 190.

11. Ibid., 192.

12. Hitchcock and Johnson, *The International Style,* 33.

13. Hitchcock, Johnson and Mumford, *Modern Architecture—International Exhibition,* 114.

14. Johnson to Mrs. H. Johnson, 21 July (1930), Johnson Papers.

15. Philip Johnson (Berlin) to Mrs. Homer H. Johnson, 22 August 1930, Johnson Papers.

16. Philip Johnson (Berlin) to Mrs. Homer H. Johnson, 1 September 1930, Johnson Papers. "We" refers to Jan Ruhtenburg (a young German architect) and Johnson. This correspondence seems to disprove an unsigned note in the Mies van der Rohe Archive, MoMA, N.Y., that suggests that J. B. Neumann introduced Johnson to Mies.

17. The proposed committee was never actually convened. Neither Reber nor Mrs. Rockefeller ever attended any planning meetings, although Reber continued to sit on the committee in an honorary position and W. W. Norton was added in a similar role. Goodyear was not involved beyond the initial planning. Stephen Clark, a museum trustee, was eventually named chairman and Samuel Lewisohn, the secretary of the Board of Trustees, was named the committee's treasurer. Both were little involved after the early stages. Lewis Mumford was also listed as a committee member in the exhibition catalogue. His participation is discussed in part 6.

18. Budget figures from the museum's exhibitions cannot be published. However, the first budget estimate (the highest of a number of successive estimates) was not as high as the sixty-eight thousand dollars figure cited by Barr in the 1970s (Lynes, *Good Old Modern,* 87), and the actual costs were much lower.

19. The museums who hosted the subsequent traveling exhibition were referred to as "subscribers" (Hitchcock, Johnson, and Mumford, *Modern Architecture—International Exhibition,* 3).

20. Hitchcock and Johnson, *The International Style,* 21.

21. Bel Geddes's competition design for the State Theater at Kharkov in the Ukraine was an award winner and was subsequently published in the United States. The curators appear to have been under the impression that the Bowman Brothers had executed some projects. See part 6.

22. Johnson, "The Architectural Exhibition," 10 February 1931, Museum Archives, MoMA, N.Y.

23. Catherine Bauer to Lewis Mumford, 9 February 1931, Mumford Papers, University of Pennsylvania.

24. Alfred H. Barr Jr., "The Necco Factory," *The Arts* (May 1928): 292–95.

25. Barr visited Weissenhof in March 1928 (Rona Roob, "The Years 1902–1929," *The New Criterion,* special issue [Summer 1987]: 16). Johnson saw the colony during the summer of 1929. It is not certain when Hitchcock first visited Stuttgart, but it was before 1930.

26. Johnson to Mumford, 3 January 1931, Mumford Papers, University of Pennsylvania.

27. Bauer to Mumford, 9 February 1931, Mumford Papers, University of Pennsylvania.

28. Mies van der Rohe to Le Corbusier, 1 February 1929, Fondation Le Corbusier, as translated in Richard Pommer and Christian Otto, *Weissenhof 1927 and the Modern Movement in Architecture* (Chicago: University of Chicago Press, 1991), 149.

29. "We have more in common than you are willing to admit—our chief difference being that it pleases me to look for a warming—if that is the word I want—or enriching of architecture—*au delà de* Le Corbusier and not before him *chez* Wright" (Hitchcock to Mumford, 21 June 1929, Mumford Papers, University of Pennsylvania.) The above quotation is also cited by Robert Wojtowicz in his 1989 presentation to the Society of Architectural Historians (Boston). For further information on the ongoing relationship of Hitchcock and Mumford see Wojtowicz's "Lewis Mumford: The Architectural Critic as Historian" in *The Architectural Historian in America,* E. B. MacDougall, ed. (Washington, D.C.: National Gallery of Art, 1990), 237–49.

Endnotes (p. 28 to p. 35)

Part Three

1. The formal committee apparently met only during the early stages of the planning. There are three sets of minutes (8 January, 17 January and 23 January 1931) in the Museum Archives, MoMA, N.Y.

2. The Smithsonian Competition, 1940; National Defense Poster Competition, 1941; United Hemisphere Poster Competition, 1942; Hidden Talent Competition, 1949; Polio Poster Competition, 1949; and Prize Designs for Modern Furniture, 1950; are listed in Department of Architecture and Design Archives, MoMA, N.Y.

3. Alfred H. Barr Jr., "Notes on Russian Architecture," *The Arts* 15, no. 2 (February 1929): 103–6, 144, 146 (citation from 103–4.)

4. Philip Johnson to Richard Neutra, 26 October 1931, Museum Archives, MoMA, N.Y.

5. "Now, the plan is the generator, the plan is the determination of everything." Le Corbusier, *Towards a New Architecture* (New York: Payson & Clarke, 1927), 144. Le Corbusier's emphasis on plans is frequently cited by the curators in their published works from this period although there are no plans in Hitchcock's *Modern Architecture*.

6. Hitchcock and Johnson, *The International Style*, 86.

7. Hitchcock, *Modern Architecture*, 204.

8. Thomas S. Hines, *Richard Neutra and the Search for Modern Architecture* (New York: Oxford University Press, 1982), 99.

9. Johnson to Mrs. H. Johnson, 21 July 1930, Johnson Papers. Anti–skyscraper sentiment is prominent in almost all of the articles that Hitchcock and Barr wrote concerning American architecture during the late twenties and early thirties. Barr's comments from "The Necco Factory" article are typical: "The skyscraper . . . is the most flagrant example of confusion and dearth of architectural imagination. Nothing is more characteristic or more vain than American pride in skyscraper architecture. Height, sheer ostentatious verticality, is good advertising but it does not make architecture, even though it has immense potentialities" (293).

10. Hitchcock, Johnson and Mumford, *Modern Architecture—International Exhibition,* 180.

11. In a subsequent revision "2%" is substituted for "25%." It is most likely that "2%" is correct and refers to the long-term annual return that an insurance company or other large mortgage holder might expect to receive from a rental property financed with government subsidies. A 25 percent return on a commercial development of low-cost housing would have actually been a very good return.

12. Philip Johnson to J.J.P. Oud, 16 April 1932, Museum Archives, MoMA, N.Y. It is not intended to infer that Hitchcock and Barr were not interested in the technical aspects of architectural production (see Searing, "Henry–Russell Hitchcock: The Architectural Historian as Critic and Connoisseur," for a discussion of Hitchcock's technical background as a student at the Fogg). However, Johnson's interest in the Taylorization of architectural production is an interest new to the curators' previously published positions.

13. Johnson to Mumford, 3 January 1931, Mumford Papers, University of Pennsylvania.

14. Lynes, *Good Old Modern,* 33.

15. In light of Johnson's subsequent political adventurism it is difficult to write reportorially of the more personal aspects of his involvement with the exhibition without misleading the reader by omission. Johnson's associations during the mid– to late 1930s with right-wing politics in the United States and Germany cast a shadow over his activities. Suffice it to say that this essay amplifies one moment in Johnson's life, a moment which was and continues to be one of seminal importance in the development of modern architecture in America. It is, however, an incomplete account and needs to be seen as part of a larger history that scholarship can and should provide.

16. Philip Johnson to Mies van der Rohe, undated draft (March 1931), Mies van der Rohe Archive, MoMA, N.Y.

17. Johnson to Mrs. H. Johnson, 21 July 1930, Johnson Papers.

18. Ibid. [emphasis added].

19. Johnson mentions Oud to his mother in a letter: "If we ever, ever build, I would have perfect confidence in him even on the other side of the ocean, something which I can not say of Corbusier" (20 June 1930). Johnson discusses the project with Oud soon thereafter and Oud responds: "I think I could do now a big thing after so many experiences with other things and it must be 'herrlich.' To make important buildings in good material, to make 'Raum' has also to do something with architecture and until now the 'Raum' I could make were nearly only streets: interesting also of course but it has to be combined with 'Raum' inside also and the labourer dwellings of very low prices are not the best objects for this" (J.J.P. Oud to Philip Johnson, 12 November 1930, Registrar's Archive, MoMA, N.Y.).

20. Philip Johnson to J.J.P. Oud, 17 March 1932, Museum Archives, MoMA, N.Y.

21. It is not clear whether the Johnsons seriously considered Clauss & Daub for the Pinehurst project or whether Johnson encouraged them to use the program as a propaganda piece. It was published in the November 1931 issue of *Architectural Record* and displayed at the "Rejected Architects" exhibition. In addition to the Pinehurst proposal, Clauss & Daub exhibited a house for the "Mrs. Charles Lindberg," which apparently had not been commissioned and drew an angry letter from Delano & Aldrich, who had been commissioned by the Lindbergs to design their house (Philip Johnson to Delano and Aldrich, 3 February 1932, Museum Archives, MoMA, N.Y.).

22. Johnson's attempt to purchase some of Le Corbusier's drawings was unsuccessful: "He had some plans to sell at what I thought would be around a hundred dollars, so we dickered and dickered only to find out that he was talking dollars and I francs." (Johnson to Mrs. H. Johnson, 20 June 1930, Johnson Papers). Some of the pieces of furniture purchased that summer can be seen in photographs of Johnson's apartment that appeared in the exhibition and in *The International Style* and are now part of the museum's permanent collection. The Mondrian painting (*Composition,* 1925)

is also part of the museum's collection and was purchased on Johnson's behalf out of Mondrian's studio by Hitchcock.

23. Johnson to Mrs. H. Johnson, 6 August 1930, Johnson Papers.

24. Pommer and Otto, *Weissenhof 1927,* 163.

25. Philip Johnson to J.J.P. Oud, 17 September 1930, Johnson Papers. See also Schulze, *Mies van der Rohe,* 185–87, regarding the architect's resistance to Nazi interference in the school.

26. R. Buckminster Fuller, *4D Time Lock* (Albuquerque: Lama Foundation, 1970), 27 (originally published privately in 1928 as *4D Philosophy, an Aphoristic Essay.)*

27. Ibid., 3.

28. Philip Johnson to Bowman Brothers, 19 March 1931, Museum Archives, MoMA, N.Y.

29. Homer Johnson's relationship with the Aluminum Company dates to its earliest days. In exchange for an interest in the enterprise he filed the patent papers for an aluminum extraction process on behalf of the cash–strapped inventors. The Aluminum Company was later renamed the Aluminum Corporation of America (ALCOA).

30. "I am very keen on getting good modern busses [sic.] and when I get back will know what one ought to look like. I would not use Lescaze but if it is impossible to work with an architect who is not in the country, then Lescaze is the only possible. My idea would be Mies. I know his office. He has all kinds of technical and economic people, and is now doing an airplane so he ought to know how to work out a technical thing like busses"[sic.] (Johnson to Mrs. H. Johnson, 1 September 1930, Johnson Papers). Lescaze had designed a bus terminal in New York City (1928) that was published in the catalogue (150); it isn't certain that Mies was ever involved in any serious project for an airplane.

31. "Thank you for getting me in touch with van der Leeuw. I was fortunately able to reach him for a luncheon at Mrs. Rockefeller's on the last day" (Johnson to

Richard Neutra, 26 May 1931, Museum Archives, MoMA, N.Y.).

32. Philip Johnson (Berlin) to Alfred H. Barr Jr. (Paris), undated (August 1931), Museum Archives, MoMA, N.Y.

33. Johnson to Mrs. H. Johnson, 7 July 1930, Johnson Papers.

34. Philip Johnson to J.J.P. Oud, 30 August (1931), Museum Archives, MoMA, N.Y. (Bruenn is the German name for Brno, Czechoslovakia, the site of the Tugendhat House.)

35. Johnson to Mrs. H. Johnson, 6 August 1930, Johnson Papers.

36. "With the Aluminum Company and with private people I have tried to arrange work for you. In January a prominent New Yorker, wishing to have his apartment done, on my recommendation alone, was willing to pay for your passage and to engage you to do this work" (Johnson to Mies [March 1931], Museum Archives, MoMA, N.Y.) The prominent New Yorker was, despite the gender reference, Mrs. Abby Rockefeller and the commission was to design an art gallery for her New York apartment. The commission went to Donald Deskey.

37. Johnson did not, however, pay for the entire exhibition as indicated in Calvin Tomkin's essay "Profiles: Forms Under Light," *The New Yorker,* 23 May 1977.

38. "I got father's letter on the boat. . . . He may rest assured I have no more intention of doing any building at this my youthful age. There are too many problems I should like to work out first. The strategic time is later, though if I had all the money in the world I would just build continuously, keep on experimenting" (Johnson to Mrs. H. Johnson, 20 June [1930], Johnson Papers).

39. "The Museum of Modern Art and Columbia University would like to invite you to come to this country for two months in late winter or early spring to give lectures and perhaps to work with international students" (Philip Johnson to J.J.P. Oud, 23 November 1933, Museum Archives, MoMA, N.Y.). This was Johnson's second attempt to get Oud to come to America. Oud's first response apparently did not discourage

Johnson's efforts: "What about the business you wrote me about? I am not a man for teaching and also a 'princely salary.' I like the real work of 'building' and only if I could get building—possibilities by it I should think a bit of teaching—a little. Naturally it would be another question to work a month or so with students on projects. But lecturing as a rule in schools and so—Brrr!" (J.J.P. Oud to Philip Johnson, 3 May 1932, Museum Archives, MoMA, N.Y.).

40. The exhibited architects were younger practitioners whose work was not accepted in the 1931 Architectural League annual exhibition: Clauss & Daub, Stonorov & Morgan, Hazen Sise, William Muschenheim, Walter Baermann, Elroy Webber and Richard Wood. The exhibition was held in a Sixth Avenue storefront owned by Julian Levy's father. See Stern, Gilmartin and Mellins, *New York 1930,* for further references.

41. The organization seems to have had only one formal meeting on 25 January 1932. The Temporary Committee is listed in the minutes (File 8036, Mumford Papers, University of Pennsylvania) as Alfred Clauss, Philip Johnson, Alfred Kastner, Norman Rice and Richard C. Wood. Other attendees listed are Catherine Bauer, Walter Baerman, Simon Brines, George Daub, Albert Frey, Henry–Russell Hitchcock, K. Lundberg–Holm, George Howe, Percival Goodman, Frederic Kiesler, John Moore, William Muschenheim, Lyman Paine, Norman Rice, Lewis Stone, Kenneth Stowell and Julian Whittlesey. The principal business discussed at the first meeting were plans for an exhibition in April of that year and a long discussion about the group and its purpose. Catherine Bauer provides a somewhat critical account of the evening: "I confined myself (almost) to an occasional sneering: 'but *is* it a group?' But I don't mean to be *quite* so nasty . . . it wasn't altogether disheartening to see so many people ready to fight for something, even though they hadn't the faintest idea what (except that in some way every sentence of their public credo must be worded so as to convey to Mr. Hood that not if he came on his hands and knees would he be allowed in.") (Catherine Bauer to Lewis Mumford, 16 January 1932, Mumford Papers, University of Pennsylvania.)

Endnotes (p. 40 to p. 48)

42. Pommer and Otto, *Weissenhof 1927*, 163.

43. Citations to this effect are unusually unequivocal: "Hitchcock and Johnson were required by the Director and the Board of Trustees to devote fifty percent of the exhibition to American architects" (Wodehouse, *The Roots of the International Style*, 131). "In order to meet the trustees' demand that there be work by a similar number of American and foreign architects." (Stern, Gilmartin, & Mellin, *New York 1930*, 344). The minutes of the Board of Trustees make no reference to any discussion of the issue, although in later years the trustees debated the museum's critics who believed that too many exhibitions were devoted to European painters. Although I have refrained in this research from citing Johnson's memory sixty years after the fact, in this instance I believe it is important to add that he has no recollection of any action by the trustees in this regard (interview with Philip Johnson, 6 November 1991).

44. Johnson to Bowman Brothers, 19 March 1931, Museum Archives, MoMA, N.Y.

45. Philip Johnson to J.J.P. Oud, 16 April 1932, Museum Archives, MoMA, N.Y. It should also be added that it would have been very difficult to have an exhibition in America of the world's "greatest" architects without including Wright. His exclusion would have been particularly difficult considering the involvement of Mumford, Wright's critical champion.

46. In *Good Old Modern* Lynes cites the Bullock's presentation but not the Chicago venue (88).

47. Johnson to Bowman Brothers, 22 May 1931, MoMA, N.Y.

48. The "large catalogue," "special reports" and "guide" to the exhibition are mentioned in various documents, including a detailed budget dated 29 April 1931, Museum Archives, MoMA, N.Y.

49. It is questionable whether or not Hitchcock considered "the style" as having the global mandate that has been ascribed to it. In a letter to Mumford on his just-published *The Brown Decades*

Hitchcock acknowledges the correctness of Mumford's position on Sullivan but maintains that Mumford's position (an emphasis on local and regional influences) is not alien to his own. Hitchcock notes: "Much you have doubtless said before I come to by a new route . . . in Le Corbusier and Mies. Localism and use of rubble stone in L.C.'s new villa near Hyères, marble and wood and straw matting in all of Mies' new work" (Henry–Russell Hitchcock to Lewis Mumford, 5 November 1931, Mumford Papers, University of Pennsylvania). Also, Hitchcock remarks in *The International Style*: "this new style is not international in the sense that the production of one country is just like that of another" (21).

50. Johnson, "The Proposed Architectural Exhibition for the Museum of Modern Art," undated (December 1930), Museum Archives, MoMA, N.Y.

Part Four

1. A ledger sheet in the Museum Archives indicates that Barr's recollection in the 1970s that Mrs. Rockefeller and Stephen Clark each contributed ten thousand dollars is not correct (Lynes, *Good Old Modern,* 87; repeated in Wodehouse, *The Roots of International Style Architecture*, footnote 1, p. xiii). The trustees' total contributions were substantially less than that sum.

2. Johnson to Mies, undated (March 1930), Museum Archives, MoMA, N.Y.

3. Philip Johnson, *Built To Live In* (New York; Museum of Modern Art, 1931), privately circulated edition of five hundred copies.

4. The Buffalo Fine Arts Academy and the Albright Art Gallery were combined and subsequently renamed the Albright–Knox Art Gallery. The Pennsylvania Museum of Art was subsequently renamed the Philadelphia Museum of Art.

5. This quotation from the 11 March 1932 minutes of the Board of Trustees was provided by the Museum Archives.

6. Bel Geddes apparently fell out favor with Johnson during this time, possibly due to his participation in the Architectural League

annual exhibition: "The trips of Norman Bel Geddes and Joseph Urban to Europe have made ribbon windows the mode, even if these men have never fully understood the new architecture" (Philip Johnson, "Rejected Architects," *Creative Art* 8, no. 6 [June 1931]: 435).

7. Philip Johnson, "The Architecture of the New School," *The Arts* 17, no. 6 (March 1931): 393–98.

8. Philip Johnson, "The Skyscraper School of Modern Architecture, *The Arts* 17, no. 8 (May 1931): 569–75.

9. Ibid., 569.

10. Checklist, "The Exhibition of Modern Architecture" file, Registrar's Archives, Philadelphia Museum of Art, Philadelphia.

11. Johnson, "Rejected Architects," *Creative Art* 8, no. 6 (June 1931): 433–35.

12. Ibid., 434. Ely Jacques Kahn was the president of the Architectural League. Deems Taylor, who was himself a musician and wrote mostly about music, apparently reviewed the exhibition, although it is not known for which publication. Douglas Haskell reviewed both the "Rejected Architects" and the League exhibitions ("The Column, the Gable and Box," *The Arts* 17, no. 9 [June 1931]: 636–39).

13. Philip Johnson to the Bowman Brothers, 22 May 1931, Museum Archives, MoMA, N.Y.

14. "I should have preferred a skyscraper model since I am convinced that you have built by far the most successful ones and may I tell you how much I like the McGraw–Hill Building? It is much better than any picture of it. Only the motif at the top strikes me as unnecessarily decorative. Another reason for having you do a skyscraper is that it will be the only one and our Show must go to Europe" (Philip Johnson to Raymond Hood, 27 May 1931, Museum Archives, MoMA, N.Y.).

15. Johnson to Neutra, 26 May 1931, Museum Archives, MoMA, N.Y.

Part Five

1. Alan Blackburn to Howe & Lescaze, 8 July 1931, Museum Archives, MoMA, N.Y.

2. J.J.P. Oud, to Philip Johnson, 18 January 1932, Museum Archives, MoMA, N.Y.

3. J.J.P. Oud to Philip Johnson, 14 October 1931, Museum Archives, MoMA, N.Y.

4. Alfred H. Barr Jr. (Paris) to Philip Johnson (Berlin), 17 July 1931, Museum Archives, MoMA, N.Y.

5. See Philip Johnson (Berlin) to Alfred Barr (Paris), 22 July 1931, Museum Archives, MoMA, N.Y.

6. See Philip Johnson (Berlin) to Alfred Barr (Austria), 7 August 1931, Museum Archives, MoMA, N.Y.

7. "von der siedlung in kassel ist ein gutes modell vorhanden, das anlässlich des internationalen kongresses in frankfurt am main ausgestellt war [sic]" (Otto Haesler to Philip Johnson [Berlin], 12 June 1931, Museum Archives, MoMA, N.Y.). Haesler is referring, most likely, to the 1929 CIAM conference in Frankfurt on minimal dwelling.

8. As cited in Hines, *Richard Neutra and the Search for Modern Architecture,* 102. Van der Leeuw to Richard Neutra, 2 June 1931, Dione Neutra Papers, (personal papers).

9. Alfred H. Barr Jr. (Paris) to Philip Johnson (Berlin), 19 August 1931, Museum Archives, MoMA, N.Y.

10. Hitchcock and Johnson, *The International Style,* 54.

11. Philip Johnson to J.J.P. Oud, 17 September 1930, Johnson Papers (apparently this letter was never mailed).

12. Charles, Comte de Noailles, to Alfred H. Barr Jr. (Paris), 11 July 1931, Museum Archives, MoMA, N.Y.

13. Hitchcock and Johnson, *The International Style,* 54–55.

14. Henry–Russell Hitchcock to Lewis Mumford, 9 June 1931, Mumford Papers, University of Pennsylvania.

15. Johnson to Barr, 7 August 1931, Museum Archives, MoMA, N.Y.

16. See Hitchcock to Mumford, 5 November 1931, University of Pennsylvania. In the *Roots of International Style Architecture,* Wodehouse suggests incorrectly that the catalogue preceded the book: "The exhibition and catalogue were followed that same year by the publication of a book . . ." (p. xvi).

17. For a more complete understanding of the development and transformation of the European modern movement see Pommer and Otto, *Weissenhof 1927.*

18. Hitchcock and Johnson, *The International Style,* 38.

19. Philip Johnson (Berlin) to Alan Blackburn, 15 August 1931, Museum Archives, MoMA, NY.

20. Johnson to Oud, 30 August 1931, MoMA, NY.

Part Six

1. Philip Johnson to Alan Blackburn, 28 July 1931, Museum Archives, MoMA, N.Y.

2. Philip Johnson to Bowman Brothers, 17 September 1931, Museum Archives, MoMA, N.Y.

3. "[Wright] told me that there were two models that were being prepared of which I could have my choice. . . . Of the two projects . . . I prefer that of the house. As Mr. Wright described it, it would be better than the theater" (Philip Johnson to Henry Klumb [Taliesin], 5 October 1931, Museum Archives, MoMA, N.Y.).

4. See Frank Lloyd Wright to Philip Johnson, 5 January 1932, Museum Archives, MoMA, N.Y.

5. Alan Blackburn to Philip Johnson (Berlin), 18 August 1931, Museum Archives, MoMA, N.Y.

6. Philip Johnson (Berlin) to Alan Blackburn, 19 August 1931, Museum Archives, MoMA, N.Y.

7. Philip Johnson to William Lescaze, 23 October 1931, Museum Archives, MoMA, N.Y.

8. Philip Johnson to Bowman Brothers, 8 October 1931, Museum Archives, MoMA, N.Y. The essays were not included in the catalogue. Irving Bowman's essay did appear in the February 1932 issue of *T-Square* (vol. 2, no. 2, 19). Howe's presentation at the Architects' Symposium (see part 7) may have grown out of his essay.

9. Johnson, "The Architectural Exhibition," 10 February 1931, Museum Archives, MoMA, N.Y.

10. Hitchcock, Johnson and Mumford, *Modern Architecture—International Exhibition*, page #11.

11. Lewis Mumford to Frank Lloyd Wright, 23 January 1932, Mumford Papers, University of Pennsylvania.

12. The Regional Planning Association advocated such "innovative planning concepts as the residential superblock, the separation of pedestrian and vehicular traffic, and the 'Townless Highway.' [Mumford] was also the most effective propagandist for the group's new housing developments in Sunnyside, Queens, and in Radburn, New Jersey. Both developments were designed by members Henry Wright and Clarence Stein" (Wojtowicz, unpublished presentation, 5). Both Sunnyside and Radburn were exhibited in the Housing section.

13. "Catherine Bauer has been writing captions for the housing section" (Lewis Mumford to Frank Lloyd Wright, 6 February 1932, Mumford Papers, University of Pennsylvania).

14. "*Our* Superslum thesis was neatly proved by every worried lady I talked to" [emphasis added], (Catherine Bauer to Lewis Mumford, undated, [January 1932], Mumford Papers, University of Pennsylvania).

15. Mumford to Wright, 6 February 1932, Mumford Papers, University of Pennsylvania.

Endnotes (p. 61 to p. 76)

16. Mumford had not visited the European projects until after the exhibition. Catherine Bauer saw the work of Oud, Gropius and May in 1930 (Wojtowicz, unpublished presentation, 5).

17. Johnson, like many members of the educated upper class, had a certain paternalistic sympathy with the plight of the impoverished working class, although this sympathy rarely involved a critique of the financial and social status quo. Before proposing his plans for involving industry and capital in solving the housing crisis Johnson made the following observation: "And now I notice that Hoover is to appoint a committee to see about building some Siedlungen, at least that is what our papers tell us. I hope that it is true and that they will study the American situation as regards the housing of the worker. But isn't it rather socialistic of our dear president. The US Government to build houses! I only hope they do" (Johnson [Berlin] to Mrs. H. Johnson, 6 August 1930, Johnson Papers).

18. Lewis Mumford to Frank Lloyd Wright, 15 September 1931, Mumford Papers, University of Pennsylvania.

19. Mumford to Wright, 6 February 1932, Mumford Papers, University of Pennsylvania. This letter is quite long and I have tried to excerpt it as faithfully as possible. Nevertheless, it is a crucial document in the relationship between Mumford and Wright and reference to the original, in toto, is recommended for anyone interested in more comprehensive study of the critical positions of both figures.

20. "Enclosed are all but one of the photos you selected yesterday" (Helen Block, Soviet Photo Agency, to Philip Johnson, 11 December 1931, Museum Archives, MoMA, N.Y.).

21. In The International Style the authors acknowledge Neutra's contribution of photographs of the Japanese project published therein.

22. Philip Johnson to Paul Nelson, 9 January 1932, Museum Archives, MoMA, N.Y.

Part Seven

1. Wodehouse's footnote indicating that the museum remained in the Heckscher Building until 1939 is incorrect (Wodehouse, The Roots of International Style Architecture, note 1, p. xiii). In 1932 the museum was relocated in a townhouse on 53rd Street until the current building was erected.

2. Exhibition Albums, 1929–1932, Photographic Archives, MoMA, N.Y.

3. "Show Modern Art Here Tomorrow," New York Times, 6 November 1929.

4. New York City Department of Buildings, Microfilm Files, N.Y.

5. The partitions screening the north window wall were modified after the museum's opening. Panel doors were constructed, presumably to ventilate the galleries.

6. "The walls are faced with monk's cloth of a neutral though warm beige" (M. S. Barr, "Our Campaigns," 23).

7. Ibid.

8. Helen Searing, "From the Fogg to the Bauhaus: A Museum for the Machine Age" in Avery Memorial Wadsworth Athenaeum, The First Modern Museum, E. Gaddis, ed. (Hartford: Wadsworth Athenaeum, 1982), 19–64.

9. The names and letters denoting the various rooms of the museum are taken from the post–installation memorandum.

10. Undated shipping memorandum (pre–installation), Museum Archives, MoMA, N.Y. The catalogue records Section One as "The Extent of Modern Architecture" and Section Two as "Modern Architects"— inexplicably, the reverse of the actual sequence and labeling of the exhibition. Stern, Gilmartin and Mellin cite the catalogue in describing the exhibition (New York 1930, 344).

11. Hitchcock and Johnson, The International Style, 54.

12. Barr, "Notes on Russian Architecture," 106.

13. Hitchcock, Johnson and Mumford, Modern Architecture—International Exhibition, 38.

14. "Median asking price for existing homes, Washington, D.C., 1932: $6,515." Historical Statistics of the United States, (Washington, D.C.: Dept. of Commerce, 1976) Table N 259–261, Price Indexes for 1 Family Houses: 1890 to 1947.

15. Alan Blackburn to Howe & Lescaze, 8 July 1931, Museum Archives, MoMA, N.Y.

16. Johnson, "The Architectural Exhibition," 10 February 1931, Museum Archives, MoMA, N.Y.

17. Philip Johnson (Berlin) to Alfred Barr (Paris), 11 July 1931, Museum Archives, MoMA, N.Y.

18. Wijdeveld supervised the installations of the various venues of the Wright exhibit that was touring Europe the summer of 1930. Wijdeveld sent Wright an album with installation photographs (Wijdeveld Album, microfilm cat. no. 1140.022, Getty Center, Los Angeles).

19. Johnson, "Memorandum," 24 September 1931, Museum Archives, MoMA, N.Y.

20. Of the museum's preferred way of installing paintings, Marga Barr writes: "The pictures are hung much lower than in any museum or commercial gallery, approximately fifty inches from the floor to the center of the picture" and "the old–fashioned system of 'skying'—hanging pictures one above the other—is nefarious. The visitor must see the works clearly and as much as possible at eye level" (M. S. Barr, "Our Campaigns," 24).

21. Johnson was not limited technically to the thirty-six-inch-high enlargements. Frank Lloyd Wright had used eight-by-eight-foot enlargements in exhibitions of his work (interview with Bruce Brooks Pfeiffer, Frank Lloyd Wright Foundation Archivist, 20 November 1991).

22. Johnson to Barr, 7 August 1931, Museum Archives, MoMA, N.Y.

23. Before the photographs were shipped the labels were attached directly to the photographs, flush with the bottom edge.

24. A text identical to one of Section Three's wall texts was published in the April 1932 issue of *Shelter* devoted to Exhibition 15. The text is not attributed but was presumably taken from the exhibition.

While in most cases the literary documentation regarding Exhibition 15 is voluminous, there are regrettable gaps. Barr and Johnson made carbons of all of their outgoing correspondence and filed and saved incoming correspondence. Unfortunately, it seems that Barr and Johnson did not correspond frequently with Hitchcock or Mumford. As the latter were frequent visitors to New York, it appears that most of their interchanges with Barr and Johnson were face–to–face encounters of which there are no records. Furthermore, I have been told by Moisette Broderick, the executor of Hitchcock's literary estate, that Hitchcock's papers at the American Archives of Art, still a closed archive, contain no additional references to Exhibition15.

After Exhibition 15 closed the entire museum was moved to West 53rd Street, which may explain some of the confusion in the photographic documentation of the exhibition. Albums 15–1 and 15–2 in the Photographic Archives (which are supposed to be the museum's visual record of the exhibition) were assembled long after the fact, possibly two years after the exhibition closed. They include photographs of projects that were not built at the time of the exhibition and photographs that appear in the book and catalogue but were not actually exhibited. As with the text panels, a number of photographs from the Housing Section are missing.

25. Johnson to Neutra, 26 October 1931, Museum Archives, MoMA, N.Y.

26. A brief survey of issues of *Architectural Record* from the period yields a host of names: Van Ojen is credited for most of Oud's photography, the Chicago Architectural Photography Company for the Robie House, Kamman for the van Nelle factory, Lucia Moholy for some of the Bauhaus photographs, Garrison for the Thompson and Churchill office building, G. S. Lance for Clauss & Daub's filling station, M. C. Jorgenson for Duiker's open–air school and W. D. Morgan for Neutra's Jardinette apartments.

27. "(Every project included) is absolutely new. Nothing that has ever been shown before in America is included" (Philip Johnson to Delano & Aldrich, 3 February 1932, Registrar's Archive, MoMA, N.Y.).

28. The Villa Savoye model was made by M. Pissarro, rue Invalides, Paris. The models of the Villa Savoye and Tugendhat House remain in the museum's permanent collections. In 1979 a replica of the Bauhaus model was commissioned by the museum, and the original maquettte was deaccessioned and given to the Bauhaus Archives, Berlin. Wright's House on the Mesa model was damaged repeatedly during the exhibition tour and like the rest of the American models was returned to the architect. Nevertheless, the models' whereabouts are unknown, according to various scholars familiar with the material.

29. Hitchcock, Johnson and Mumford, *Modern Architecture—International Exhibition*, 8-9.

30. Stephen C. Clark to Herbert Hoover, 28 November 1931, Museum Archives, MoMA, N.Y.

31. Catherine Bauer to Lewis Mumford, 29 January 1932, Mumford Papers, University of Pennsylvania. It should also be noted that Bauer wrote a very positive review of the exhibition (Catherine Bauer, "Exhibition of Modern Architecture at the Museum of Modern Art," *Creative Art* [March 1932]: 201-6).

32. Alfred H. Barr Jr. to Henry-Russell Hitchcock, 13 February 1932, Museum Archives, MoMA, N.Y.

33. Royal Cortissoz, "Architecture: The Turn It Is Taking Under Modernistic Hands," *New York Herald Tribune*, 14 February 1932.

34. The April 1932 issue of *Shelter* (2, no. 3 [April 1932]: 1–29) was devoted largely to Exhibition 15. Howe, Hitchcock, Barr and Johnson were associate editors of the issue. Howe had been involved with the magazine since its inception; Hitchcock and Barr were guest editing and Johnson had recently invested in the magazine and was briefly working on its editorial board.

35. Alfred H. Barr, Jr. to Lewis Mumford, 13 February 1932, Museum Archives, MoMA, N.Y.

36. "Symposium: The International Architectural Exhibition," *Shelter* 2, no. 3 (April 1932): 3–4.

37. Form letter dated 4 March 1932, signed Alfred H. Barr, Jr., Museum Archives, MoMA, N.Y.

38. Hitchcock and Johnson, *The International Style* (1966 ed.), xii.

39. Philip Johnson to J.J.P. Oud, 17 March 1932, Museum Archives, MoMA, N.Y.

40. Stern, Gilmartin and Mellins, *New York 1930*, 329–55 ("Exhibitions").

41. Suzanne Stephens, ed., *Skyline* (February 1982): 24–27.

42. Bauer to Mumford, 29 January 1932, Mumford Papers, University of Pennsylvania.

43. "Miniature Apartment Dwellings to be Included in Display at Wadsworth," *Hartford Courant*, 22 April 1932.

44. Ibid.

45. Susan Murray, "International Type Architecture to Be Shown at Morgan," *Hartford Times*, 21 April 1932. In fairness, it should be noted that this article is generally stronger than the citation excerpted.

46. "Modern Architecture at Art Museum," *Sunday Telegram* (Worcester, Mass.), 18 June 1933.

47. Murray, "International Type Architecture."

48. Henry-Russell Hitchcock, "Architectural Criticism," *Shelter* 2, no. 3 (April 1932): 2.

Endnotes (p. 87 to p. 95)

49. "The text seems to me (as far as I read it) excellent. The school mastering under the illustrations I don't like" (J.J.P. Oud to Philip Johnson, 6 April 1932, Museum Archives, MoMA, N.Y.).

50. R. M. Schindler to Philip Johnson, 9 March 1932, Museum Archives, MoMA, N.Y.

51. Frank Lloyd Wright to Philip Johnson, 18 January 1932, Museum Archives, MoMA, N.Y. It should be noted that it is not clear from the preceding nor the subsequent correspondence whether "amateur" and "salesman" refer to the curators or Wright's colleagues.

52. "But being in some degree essential to the propaganda, as the promoters of the exhibition see it, I have consented to go along with them if I might state my feelings in plain terms alongside their own statements. 'Of Thee I Sing' is that somewhat ungracious statement" (Frank Lloyd Wright, draft preface, 'Of Thee I Sing,' 26 February 1932, Museum Archives, MoMA, N.Y.).

53. Frank Lloyd Wright, "Of Thee I Sing," *Shelter* 2, no. 3 (April 1932): 10–12.

54. K. Londberg-Holm, "Two Shows: A Comment on the Aesthetic Racket," Arthur T. North, "Old New Stuff" and Chester Aldrich, "Modernism and Publicity," *Shelter* 2, no. 3 (April 1932): 16–17, 12–16 and 24–26, respectively.

55. William Adams Delano, "Man Versus Mass," *Shelter* 2, no. 3 (April 1932): 12. Also cited in Stern, Gilmartin and Mellin's *New York 1930*.

Notes

1. For additional information see Pomer and Otto, *Weissenhof 1927*, chapter 16.

2. Hitchcock, "Four Harvard Architects," 47.

3. Calvin Tomkins, "Profiles: Forms Under Light," *The New Yorker*, 23 May 1977, 48.

4. Barr, "Notes on Russian Architecture," 105.

5. Hitchcock, *Modern Architecture*, 162.

6. Philip Johnson, lecture notes, "International Style—Death or Metamorphosis," 30 March 1961, Museum Archives, MoMA, N.Y.

7. As quoted in Alice Goldfarb Marquis, *Alfred H. Barr, Jr.—Missionary for the Modern* (Chicago: Contemporary Books, 1989), 85.

8. Hitchcock and Johnson, *The International Style*, 11.

9. Lynes, *Good Old Modern*, 87.

10. Haesler to Johnson, undated response to Johnson's letter of 2 September 1930, MoMA, N.Y.

11. Hitchcock and Johnson, *The International Style* (1966 edition), vii.

12. Johnson, "The Architecture of the New School," 393.

13. Eisenman interview, 14 and Wodehouse, *The Roots of International Style* Architecture, note 1, xiii.

14. Lynes, *Good Old Modern*, 86.

15. Irving Sandler and Amy Newman, eds., *Defining Modern Art—Selected Writings of Alfred H. Barr, Jr.* (New York: Abrams, 1986), 69.

16. "First we are going to Munich and then around to Berlin via Frankfurt. Then to Stockholm, and back, and then I shall come back for a month in Paris to learn French" (Philip Johnson [Paris] to Mrs. Homer H. Johnson [Pentecost], June 1930, Johnson Papers).

17. "Some say time at the University of Berlin, where I could get my *Kunstwissenschaft* well with Professor Goldschmitt who is a good friend of mine by now, as a second subject, with Economics my main. I could work toward a doctorate, which in Europe is something to be had by all means. I am going to matriculate anyhow this fall which won't hurt anything and will save time if I want to study later" (Johnson to Mrs. H. Johnson, 6 August 1930, Johnson Papers).

Afterword

1. Vincent Scully, "Buildings Without Souls," *New York Times*, 8 September 1985, 6: 43.

2. Hitchcock, "Architectural Criticism," 2.

3. H. H. Arnason, *The History of Modern Art* (New York: Abrams, 1968).

Select Bibliography

Aldrich, Chester. "Modernism and Publicity." *Shelter* 2, no. 3 (April 1932): 24–26.

Barr, Jr., Alfred H. "The Necco Factory." *The Arts* 13, no. 5 (May 1928): 292–295.

———. "Notes on Russian Architecture." *The Arts* 15, no. 2 (February 1929): 103–106, 144, 146.

———. "Modern Architecture." *The Hound and Horn* 3, no. 3 (April-June 1930): 431-435.

———. *Painting and Sculpture in The Museum of Modern Art—1929–1967.* New York: Museum of Modern Art, 1977.

Barr, Margaret Scolari. "Our Campaigns: 1930-1944." *New Criterion*, special issue, (Summer 1987): 23–74.

———. "Philip Johnson." Typescript of the early history of the Museum. Museum Archives, MoMA, N.Y.

Bauer, Catherine. "Exhibition of Modern Architecture at the Museum of Modern Art." *Creative Art* (March 1932): 201–6.

Cortissoz, Royal. "Architecture: The Turn It Is Taking Under Modernistic Hands." *New York Herald Tribune*, 14 February 1932.

Davison, Robert L. "The First All-Metal Apartment House." *The Architectural Record* 58, no. 1 (July 1930): 3–9.

Delano, William Adams. "Man Versus Mass." *Shelter* 2, no. 3 (April 1932): 12.

Drexler, Arthur and Hines, Thomas S. *The Architecture of Richard Neutra.* New York: Museum of Modern Art, 1982.

Drexler, Arthur. *The Mies van der Rohe Archive.* Vol. 1. New York: Garland, 1986.

Eisenman, Peter. "Interview" (with Philip Johnson). *Skyline* (February 1982): 14–17.

Fuller, R. Buckminster. *4D Time Lock.* Albuquerque: Lama Foundation, 1970. Originally published privately in 1928 as *4D Philosophy, an Aphoristic Essay.*

Hitchcock, Henry-Russell. "The Decline of Architecture." *The Hound and Horn* 1, no. 1, (September 1927): 28–35.

———. "The Architectural Work of J.J.P. Oud." *The Arts* (February 1928): 97–103.

———. "Four Harvard Architects." *The Hound and Horn* 2, no. 1 (September 1928): 41–47.

———. *Frank Lloyd Wright.* Paris: Cahiers D'Art, 1928.

———. "Dessau—July 1927." *The Architectural Record* 66, no. 8 (August 1929): 191.

———. *Modern Architecture: Romanticism and Reintegration.* New York: Payson and Clarke, 1929; reprint New York: Hacker, 1970.

———. "Berlin: Paris: 1931." *The Hound and Horn* 5, no. 1 (October-December 1931): 94–97.

———. "Architectural Criticism." *Shelter* 2, no. 3 (April 1932): 2.

Hitchcock, Henry-Russell and Johnson, Philip. *The International Style: Architecture Since 1922.* New York: W. W. Norton, 1932; reprint, 1966.

Hitchcock, Henry-Russell, Johnson, Philip and Mumford, Lewis. *Modern Architecture—International Exhibition.* New York: Museum of Modern Art, 1932. Also published as *Modern Architects.* New York: Museum of Modern Art and W. W. Norton, 1932.

Haskell, Douglas. "The Column, the Gable and the Box." *The Arts* 17, no. 9 (June 1931): 636–639.

Hines, Thomas S. *Richard Neutra and the Search for Modern Architecture.* New York: Oxford University Press, 1982.

Londberg-Holm, K. "Two Shows: A Comment on the Aesthetic Racket." *Shelter* 2, no. 3 (April 1932): 16–17.

Hubert, Christian and Shapiro, Lindsay Stamm. *William Lescaze.* New York: IAUS/Rizzoli, 1982.

Historical Statistics of the United States—Colonial Times to 1970. Washington, D.C.: Dept. of Commerce, 1976)

Jeanneret, Charles E. (Le Corbusier). *Vers Une Architecture.* Paris: G. Cres, 1927.

Johnson, Philip. "Modernism in Architecture." *The New Republic*, 18 March 1931, 134.

———. *Built To Live In.* New York; Museum of Modern Art, 1931, privately circulated edition of 500 copies.

———. "The Architecture of the New School." *The Arts* 17, no. 6 (March 1931): 393–98.

———. "The Skyscraper School of Modern Architecture." *The Arts* 17, no. 8 (May 1931): 569–75.

———. "Rejected Architects." *Creative Art* 8, no. 6 (June 1931): 433–35.

Kirsch, Karin. *The Weissenhofsiedlung.* New York: Rizzoli, 1989.

Lynes, Russell. *Good Old Modern: An Intimate Portrait of the Museum of Modern Art.* New York: Atheneum, 1973.

Mumford, Lewis. "Modern Architecture." *The New Republic*, 19 March 1930, 131–32.

North, Arthur T. "Old New Stuff." *Shelter* 2, no. 3 (April 1932): 12–16.

Bibliography (cont.)

Pommer, Richard and Otto, Christian. *Weissenhof 1927 and the Modern Movement in Architecture*. Chicago: University of Chicago Press, 1991.

Platz, Gustav. *Die Baukunst der neuesten Zeit*. Berlin: Propylaenverlag 1927; reprint 1931.

Roob, Rona. "Alfred H. Barr, Jr: A Chronicle of the Years 1902–1929." *New Criterion*, special issue (Summer 1987): 1–19.

Sandler, Irving and Newman, Amy. *Defining Modern Art: Selected Writings of Alfred H. Barr, Jr.* New York: Abrams, 1986.

Scully, Vincent. "Buildings Without Souls." *New York Times*, 8 September 1985, 6: 43.

Schulze, Franz. *Mies van der Rohe: A Critical Biography*. Chicago: University of Chicago Press, 1985.

Searing, Helen. "From the Fogg to the Bauhaus: A Museum for the Machine Age." *Avery Memorial, Wadsworth Athenaeum, The First Modern Museum*, E. Gaddis, ed. (Hartford: Wadsworth Athenaeum, 1982), 19–64.

————. "Henry-Russell Hitchcock: The Architectural Historian as Critic and Connoisseur" in *The Architectural Historian in America*, E. B. MacDougall, gen. ed., *Studies in the History of Art* 35 (Washington, D.C.: National Gallery of Art, 1990), 251–63.

Stephens, Suzanne. "Looking Back at 'Modern Architecture.'" *Skyline* (February 1982): 18–27.

Stern, Robert, Gilmartin, Gregory and Mellin, Thomas. *New York 1930: Architecture and Urbanism Between the Two World Wars*. New York: Rizzoli, 1987.

Wodehouse, Lawrence. *The Roots of International Style Architecture*. West Cornwall, Conn.: Locust Hill Press, 1991.

Wojtowicz, Robert. "Lewis Mumford: The Architectural Critic as Historian" in *The Architectural Historian in America*, E. B. MacDougall, gen. ed., *Studies in the History of Art* 35 (Washington, D.C.: National Gallery of Art, 1990), 237–49.

Wright, Frank Lloyd. "Of Thee I Sing." *Shelter* 2, no. 3 (April 1932): 10–12.

APPENDICES*

*A number of the Appendices printed here (except 3 and 4) were transcribed from originial documents in the archives of The Museum of Modern Art. They have been typeset for this publication in a manner faithful to the orignial documents but are not facsimiles. Selected typographical errors have been corrected and what is printed here does not reflect the pagination of the originals.

Appendix One: Preliminary Proposal for an Architectural Exhibition at The Museum of Modern Art
by Philip Johnson

The Proposed Architectural Exhibition for The Museum of Modern Art

The Need for an Exhibition of Modern Architecture:

There exists today both here in America and abroad a marked activity in architecture. Technical advances, new methods and fresh thoughts are solving contemporary building problems in a manner that can truly be called modern. A progressive group of architects, who have put aside traditional forms and are striking out along new and vigorous lines, are at work. In America Frank Lloyd Wright has for decades built modern houses. Raymond Hood is building the first really modern skyscrapers. Neutra's sanatorium in California, and Samuel Insull's great housing project in Chicago show the extent in the United States. Modern architecture is most widely accepted in Germany. The city of Frankfort has built tens of thousands of cheap houses. Mies van der Rohe, one of the leaders of the movement, has complete charge of the Berlin Building Exposition of 1931. The Bauhaus, a school founded by the architect Gropius, is identified with modern movements in the arts and crafts. Russia builds entirely modern. The builders of Frankfort have been recently called there to create fourteen cities in five years. In Paris many mansions are modern, and Le Corbusier is now building a large Salvation Army base there. Holland has long been a leader in the movement. Sweden in her exposition of 1930, has definitely turned away from eclecticism. From Vienna, from Helsingfors, and from Tokyo reports of modern building reach us. Every architectural magazine in the world, and even the more popular art digests carry accounts of modern architecture. Conservative architects the world over are turning to the modern style.

In view of this international recognition of what is happening in architecture, the time is opportune for an exhibition. Obviously an architecture show is by far the most effective way of presenting this important work. The hope of developing really comprehensive and intelligent criticism in both architect and public depends upon furnishing them with a knowledge of contemporary accomplishments in this field. Their sadly imperfect and limited vision is caused by the very lack of those examples which the exhibition will supply.

American architecture finds itself in a chaos of conflicting and very often unintelligent building. An introduction to an integrated and decidedly rational mode of building is sorely needed. The stimulation and direction which an exhibition of this type can give to contemporary architectural thought is incalculable.   As an example, America has for a long time sought a definite and practicable program for housing people in the lowest wage-earning class. How welcome would be a display of solutions to this problem arrived at by European and American experts!

It is desirable that our country should view and ponder the new mode of building which fits so decidedly our methods of standardized construction, our economics, and our life.

Incidentally, no little benefit will accrue to the museum in sponsoring the exhibition. In addition to the attendant publicity, a different and more varied audience will be attracted to the museum—the industrialist, the educator, the builder, the home owner.

THE PROGRAM

There will be three main divisions of the exhibition.

1. Nine of the most prominent architects of the world will be asked to present models. These architects are:

from America	Raymond Hood
	Frank Lloyd Wright
	Norman Bel Geddes
	Howe & Lescaze
	Bowman Brothers
from Germany	Mies van der Rohe
	Walter Gropius
from France	Le Corbusier
from Holland	J.J.P. Oud

Each will construct a model of that type of building best suited to his genius. Raymond Hood may choose a skyscraper, Gropius an apartment house, Bel Geddes a theater and so on. These men are chosen as representing the highest aesthetic achievements in architecture in the twentieth century. Their models will represent the forefront of development in their respective fields.

These models, invaluable as historic documents, will become the property of the museum.

Each of these men will be asked to write a comment on their respective works. This comment, together with a biographical sketch and a critical survey of their works, will appear in a special catalogue.

2. On the industrial side there will be models representing three fields of endeavor. A great builder such as Col. Starrett, of Starrett Bros. & Eken, contractors for the Empire State Building, will be asked to incorporate his most recent theories of city buildings. A great factory builder, such as the Austin Co., will prepare a model representing the most advanced development of factory design. And third, of great significance, there will be a model of an industrial housing project incorporating the most recent and scientific theory on the subject in America.

In these three models the emphasis will be placed on the problems of planning and construction rather than on finished architectural expression.

Detailed reports on the plan, construction, and cost will be prepared.

3. There will be a world-wide competition open to students and architects under thirty-five years of age. The prize will be awarded for the design of a school which is most beautiful and most completely fulfills the detailed requirements laid down by a special committee. The problem involving a school is of universal interest. Latent talent in the younger generation will be brought to the attention of architects and public alike.
To insure the maximum effectiveness of the presentation, the arrangement of the exhibition will be in the hands of Mies van der Rohe, a modern architect expert in the field.

The date of the exhibition has tentatively been set for February 1, 1932. The advantages of holding the show as soon as possible cannot be overestimated.

A publicity program, insuring the widest possible advertising for the show, is partially completed.

A budget for all expenses is being prepared. From the nature of the show the expenses will be much higher than those of the normal exhibition. A program of money raising to meet this expense is now under consideration. It is believed that because of the very widespread interest of such a show among industrialists and builders, this money can be obtained otherwise than from the Museum's budget or from friends who have hitherto been so generous.

THE DIRECTION

The direction of the show will be under the supervision of a committee. The list of members has been tentatively drawn up.

> Mr. Alfred H. Barr, Jr.
> Mr. A. Conger Goodyear
> Mr. Homer H. Johnson of Cleveland
> Mr. Philip Johnson, Sec'y.
> Dr. Reber of Lausanne, Switzerland
> Mrs. John D. Rockefeller, Jr.

Mr. Johnson has offered his full-time services for the ensuing year, and also the services of an executive secretary, Mr. Alan R. Blackburn, over the same period. The executive secretary will coordinate all the various aspects of the exhibition including all business arrangements, reports and publicity. Mr. Johnson has already also offered a business headquarters which will be constantly at the service of the committee.

WHAT HAS BEEN DONE.

In addition to the above-mentioned gift of Mr. Johnson of his time, the time of an executive secretary, and office space, much has already been accomplished which bears directly on the success of the exhibition. Mr. Johnson has devoted one year to studying the entire field both here and abroad. He has established contacts with architects, collected numerous data and photographs, and in general laid the necessary groundwork.

THE NEXT STEP.

The approval of the Trustees of the Museum is the next step.

Directly following this approval, the Committee will definitely be formed and begin its work.

Appendix Two: Revised Exhibition Proposal

February 10, 1931.
THE ARCHITECTURAL EXHIBITION
FOR THE MUSEUM OF MODERN ART IN 1932.
A Confidential Statement
by
Philip Johnson

Foreword

Never in this country or abroad has a comprehensive exhibition of modern architecture been held. It is the aim of this report to outline the need for such an exhibition, the form in which the exhibition will be presented, and also to propose the practical steps by which the program can be successfully realized.

Table of Contents

Appendix Three: Rejected Architects' Pamphlet by Philip Johnson

REJECTED ARCHITECTS

MODELS PROJETS PHOTOS

APRIL 21 - MAY 5 · 12 to 10 P.M.
OPPOSITE CARNEGIE HALL
171 W. 57th — USE 7th AVE. ENTRANCE

An Exhibition organized by architects whose models were not accepted for the current Architectural League Show at the Grand Central Palace.

CLAUSS & DAUB   Country House
                      Country House
                      Theatre for Russia
                      Housing Development
                      Boys' Club
STONOROV & MORGAN   House
                      House
HAZEN SISE   House
WILLIAM MUSCHENHEIM   Hotel
WALTER BAERMANN Photograph of an Office Interior
ELROY WEBBER   Project for Shop Front
RICHARD WOOD   House

Inquiries should be addressed to:
Clauss & Daub, 509 Fifth Avenue

In 1855 when Courbet was refused for the seventh time by the Salon, he set up his own show in a wooden shed. In 1863 Napoleon III founded the Salon des Refusés for such rebels as Manet and the Impressionists.

In 1931 a Salon des Refusés is still useful. Eight of the nine models in the exhibition of "Rejected Architects" were refused by the Architectural League.

Inspired in part by the pioneer Frank Llyod Wright, modern architecture in Europe has reached a definition of style through the work of four leaders. Le Corbusier in Paris, Oud in Rotterdam, Gropius and Mies van der Rohe in Berlin. In the last decade the style has become international. This International Style has little in common with the capricious and illogical work of the "modernistic" architects who have recently won such popularity in America. The "Rejected Architects," all of them under thirty years of age, work in the International Style. Some of them have studied with Mies or Le Corbusier.

These are the important elements in the International Style.
1. The design depends primarily on the function which the building is to serve without consideration of traditional principles of symmetry.

2. The style takes advantage of new principles of construction and new materials such as concrete, steel and glass. As a result the style is characterized by flexibility, lightness and simplicity. Ornament has no place, since hand-cut ornament is impracticable in an industrial age. The beauty of the style rests in the free composition of volumes and surfaces, the adjustments of such elements as doors and windows, and the perfection of machined surfaces.

I.   WHAT THE MUSEUM OF MODERN ART IS

        In the summer of 1929 the Museum of Modern Art was founded by a group of prominent New Yorkers who believed the art of our time was not receiving adequate presentation from existing institutions. Since the fall of the same year exhibitions have regularly been held at the Museum's quarters in the Hecksher Building, 730 Fifth Avenue, New York. The composition of the present Board of Trustees is as follows:

                        A. Conger Goodyear, President
                        Miss Lizzie [later referred to as Lillie P.] Bliss, Vice-President
                        Mrs. John D. Rockefeller, Jr., Treasurer
                        Samuel A. Lewisohn, Secretary

William T. Aldrich   Chester Dale
Frederic Clay Bartlett   Duncan Phillips
Stephen C. Clark   Mrs. Rainey Rogers
Mrs. W. Murray Crane   Paul J. Sachs
Frank Crowinshield   Mrs. Cornelius J. Sullivan

        The attached brochure briefly outlines the policy of the Museum.

II.   WHAT THE MUSEUM HAS DONE

        During the first year of its service from November 7, 1929 to November 1, 1930, 203,646 people visited the Museum. In the more important exhibitions the attendance has been as high as 50,000 in a single month.

In this brief time the Museum has attained a position of authority and prestige in the world of art. The Museum is the most important institution of its kind in America. It is believed that in the next two years it will assume the proportions of the Luxembourg in Paris and the Tate Gallery in London.

The Museum's importance extends far beyond New York as it draws upon all the important museums and collections in America, so that its activities are eagerly watched by the whole nation. Its international importance is even more evident, since over ten European museums, including the Louvre and the National Gallery in Berlin, have contributed to its exhibitions, as well as many important collectors. Several of the Museum's exhibitions have been insured for over $2,000,000.

III.   THE MUSEUM PLANS AN EXHIBITION OF MODERN ARCHITECTURE IN 1932

        The Trustees of the Museum have appointed a Committee to organize the Exhibition of Modern Architecture in 1932. The composition of this Committee is as follows:
                        Stephen C. Clark, Chairman
                        Samuel A. Lewisohn, Treasurer
                        Homer H. Johnson
                        Dr. G. F. Reber
                        Alfred Barr, Director of the Museum of Modern Art

Mr. Philip Johnson has been appointed Director of the Exhibition and the entire supervision of the Show will be in his hands.

        Never in this country or abroad has a comprehensive exhibition of Modern Architecture been held. Below is briefly outlined the need for such an exhibition and the form in which the exhibition will be presented.

THE NEED FOR AN EXHIBITION OF MODERN ARCHITECTURE

The New Architecture
        There exists today, both here in America and abroad, a marked activity in architecture. Technical advances, new methods and fresh thoughts are solving contemporary building problems in

a manner that can truly be called modern. A progressive group of architects, who have put aside traditional forms and have struck out along new and vigorous lines, are at work all over the world.

Activity in America

In America, for almost three decades, Frank Lloyd Wright has been building modern houses. The aspirations of Raymond Hood are being crystallized by the erection , after his designs, of the first really modern skyscrapers. A large house in Los Angeles, the Samuel Insull Housing Project in Chicago, a Country Day School in Philadelphia bear further witness to the widespread nature of the movement in our land.

Activity in Germany

Modern architecture is rapidly approaching national acceptance not only by the architects but also by the city governments and national government of Germany. Frankfort alone has instigated the building of thousands of efficient, low cost houses. A leader of the movement, Mies van der Rohe, President of the Werkbund, an impressive organization of German industrialists, is directing the Berlin Building Exposition of 1931. Gropius, long in the vanguard of architectural activity, has established a school with modern tenets in Dessau... the famous Bauhaus.

Activity in Russia

Russia has "gone modern" to the complete exclusion of traditional forms. She has turned to Germany and borrowed those energetic builders and planners from Frankfort, directing them to create for her fourteen cities in five years.

Activity in France

France abounds in examples of the new construction. Le Corbusier is now erecting in Paris the extensive Salvation Army headquarters at 76 Rue de Rome.

Activity in Other Countries

A glance at the other countries reveals concrete evidence of the same trend. The modern building is by no means a newcomer in Holland. Sweden moved decisively away from traditional eclecticism in her Architectural Exposition of 1930. Echoes of modern design and methods in architecture are heard from Switzerland, Czechoslovakia, Vienna, Helsingfors, and even from far-away Japan.

Recognition by Critics

Every architectural magazine in the world, and now even the more popular art digests, are devoting increasing space to modern architecture.

Recognition by Architects

Conservative architects the world over are welcoming, studying and applying the possibilities offered by the new movement.

The Time is Opportune for an Exhibition

In view of this international outburst of activity, and recognition of what is happening in architecture, the time is opportune for an exhibition. Obviously, an architectural show is by far the most effective way of presenting this important work. The hope of developing really comprehensive and intelligent criticism in both architect and public depends upon furnishing them with a knowledge of contemporary accomplishments in the field. Their sadly imperfect and limited vision is caused by the very lack of those examples which the exhibition will supply.

American architecture finds itself in a chaos of conflicting and very often unintelligent building. An introduction to an integrated and decidedly rational mode of building is sorely needed. The stimulation and direction which an exhibition of this type can give to contemporary architectural thought is incalculable. As an example, America has for a long time sought a definite and practicable program for housing our minimum wage earners, especially the factory workers. How welcome would be a display of solutions to this problem arrived at by American and European experts!

It is desirable, therefore, that our country should view and ponder the new mode of building which fits so decidedly our methods of standardized construction, our economies, and our life.

THE NATURE OF THE EXHIBITION

The Show will be divided into two main categories:

1.   Models by American and Foreign Architects.
Ten of the most prominent architects of the world will construct models of that type of building best suited to their individual genius. These men are chosen as representing the highest aesthetic achievement in twentieth century architecture. Their models will demonstrate that modern architecture has achieved expression in practically every line of building ... the home, school, railroad station, factory, apartment house, department store, civic building, prison and church.

ARCHITECTS REPRESENTING AMERICA	MODELS
Bowman Brothers	Prison
Norman Bel Geddes	Theatre
Raymond Hood	Skyscraper
Howe & Lescaze	School
Richard J. Neutra	Community Housing Project
Frank Lloyd Wright	Country Home
ARCHITECTS REPRESENTING GERMANY	
Walter Gropius	Apartment House
Mies van der Rohe	Residence
ARCHITECTS REPRESENTING FRANCE	
Le Corbusier	Department Store
ARCHITECTS REPRESENTING HOLLAND	
J.J.P. Oud	Public Building

Plans and Photographs
Explanatory plans, elevations and perspectives will be placed on the wall behind each model.

Enlarged photographs of actual buildings by these architects will also be shown.

Special Catalogues

Each architect will be invited to write a comment on his respective model. This comment, together with a biographical sketch and a critical survey of his works will appear in a special catalogue.

2.   Solutions to Three American Building Problems.

CITY BUILDING...Group Model   Colonel Starrett of Starrett Bros. & Eken

Modern Architecture seeks to extend the principles employed so successfully in the well planned house or office building to organizing groups of buildings which may cover a city block or city section. The single structures of such a group would be planned, not as isolated units, but as dependent parts of a large community. Such a community would contain within itself many functions of hotel, business offices, restaurant, theatre, etc. The advantages of this planning are: great savings by substitution of short building to building communications for round about and congested street routes, reduced construction expenses from elimination of tall buildings, and finally a general economy of avoiding duplications of function so common in the city today.

FACTORY ORGANIZATION...Factory Model...The Austin Company

Research in factory organization has led to important innovations. The model will show a windowless factory artificially lighted and ventilated.

HOUSING PROJECT FOR MINIMUM WAGE EARNERS........Model

Housing of minimum wage earners is a subject claiming the attention of the nation. Private enterprise, under existing construction methods, realizes a return of but 25% on capitol invested. The State and City governments are faced with the problem of subsidizing this type of building. The model with accompanying reports will propose a solution taking into account lower construction cost while maintaining a high standard of living conditions.

<u>Reports Accompanying These Models</u>

The preparation of detailed printed reports will be an important adjunct of this part of the exhibition. A concise, understandable presentation of plans, construction methods and costs will be prepared for easy access to those visiting the exhibition.

ARRANGEMENT AND SETTING OF THE EXHIBITION

The art of exhibiting is in itself a field of modern architecture. In view of this fact, one of the most prominent modern architects, Mies van der Rohe of Berlin, has been chosen to design the Show. His arrangement of the German exhibits at the Barcelona Exposition in 1929 won him an international reputation. He is now directing the Berlin Building Exposition of 1931.

The work of arrangement included designing bases for the models, tables for the literature, chairs, photograph racks and partition screens of glass and metal.

Though space, of course, prevents the display of any full sized work of architecture, these incidental fixtures and the furniture will show to some extent in actual objects what has been achieved in Modern Architecture.

THE DATE

The date of the Exhibition has been tentatively set for February 1, 1932. The advantages of holding the Show as soon as possible cannot be over emphasized.

ITINERARY AND PUBLICITY

The Exhibition will remain in New York eight or ten weeks and will then travel to museums in all the principal cities of the country. Judging from the keen interest abroad in new ideas in Architecture emanating from America, the unique character and selectivity of the Show will necessitate a European and Japanese itinerary.

Publicity for the Show will be extensive. Besides announcements and comments in newspapers and magazines, the general appeal of the Show, it is safe to assume, will attract further attention from Architects, Engineers, Industrialists, Builders, as well as the general public. The experimental nature of the Show coupled with its timely appearance will undoubtedly provoke lively and fruitful controversy.

Appendix 4:
Subscribers Memorandum by Philip Johnson

MEMORANDUM TO PROPOSED EXHIBITORS
AND PRELIMINARY ITINERARY

MEMORANDUM ON THE
ARCHITECTURAL EXHIBITION

September 24, 1931

MEMORANDUM ON THE ARCHITECTURAL
EXHIBITION FROM THE MUSEUM
OF MODERN ART.

1.   ITINERARY OF THE EXHIBITION.

I.   MUSEUM OF MODERN ART,
        NEW YORK.
        Opening date—Wednesday, February
        10, 1932.
        Closing date—Wednesday, March
        23, 1932.
        Number of days at Museum—43
        Number of days for shipment to next
        Museum—7.

II.   PENNSYLVANIA ART MUSEUM.
        Opening date—Wednesday, March
        30, 1932.
        Closing date —Friday, April 22, 1932.
        Number of days at Museum—24
        Number of days for shipment to next
        Museum—10.

III.   SEATTLE ART INSTITUTE.
        Opening date—Saturday, May 7, 1932.
        Closing date—Sunday, June 5, 1932.
        Number of days at Museum—30
        Number of days for shipment to next
        Museum—10

IV.   THE M. H. DE YOUNG MEMORIAL
        MUSEUM, SAN FRANCISCO.
        Opening date—Thursday, June 16,
        1932.
        Closing date—Friday, July 15, 1932.
        Number of days at Museum—30
        Number of days for shipment to next
        Museum—13

V.   LOS ANGELES MUSEUM,
        CALIFORNIA.
        Opening date—Friday, July 29, 1932.
        Closing date—Saturday, August
        27, 1932.
        Number of days at Museum—30.

VI.   BUFFALO FINE ARTS ACADEMY.
        Opening date—Thursday, September
        15, 1932.
        Closing date—Monday, October
        17, 1932.
        Number of days at Museum—33
        Number of days for shipment to next
        Museum—9

VII.   CLEVELAND MUSEUM OF ART.
        Opening date—Thursday, October
        27, 1932.
        Closing date—Sunday, December
        4, 1932.
        Number of days at Museum—30
        Number of days for shipment to next
        Museum—14.

VIII.   TOLEDO MUSEUM OF ART.
        Opening date—Monday, December
        19, 1932. Closing date —Sunday,
        January 29, 1933. Number of days at
        Museum—42. Number of days for
        shipment to next Museum—24.

IX.   CINCINNATI ART MUSEUM.
        Opening date—Wednesday, February
        22, 1933. Closing date—Thursday,
        March 23, 1933. Number of days at
        Museum—30

IX a.   MILWAUKEE ART INSTITUTE.
        February, 1933.

X.   FOGG ART MUSEUM, CAMBRIDGE,
        Mass., March, 1933.

XI.   CARNEGIE INSTITUTE, PITTSBURGH,
        Pa.—April, 1933.

XII.   ST. PAUL INSTITUTE. —May, 1933.

XIII.   ROCHESTER MEMORIAL ART
        GALLERY.—September, 1933.

XIV.   ART MUSEUM, WORCESTER
        October, 1933.

XV.   ART INSTITUTE OF OMAHA.
        November, 1933.

XVI.   MUSEUM OF FINE ARTS,
        HOUSTON, Texas.

It is important to note that all the Museums taking the Exhibition in the first year up to and including Toledo are expected to contribute $1,000 to the Exhibition, plus expenses of transportation and insurance (to be under $100.) The Museum directly following Toledo will contribute between $500 and $1,000. The other Museums following in the second year are expected to contribute $500 plus expenses (to be under $100).

2.   CONTENTS OF THE EXHIBITION.

The organization of the Exhibition is now practically complete. The foreign and American models are under construction, the photographs have been secured and the catalogue is in preparation.

(1)   MODELS:

American Models: The following American architects will be represented in the Exhibition by a model.

Eastern States
        Howe & Lescaze,
        Building Development.

        Raymond Hood, Skyscraper
        apartment house.

Middlewestern States
        Bowman Brothers, Prison.

        Frank Lloyd Wright, House

Western States
        Richard Neutra, House

Foreign Models:

Germany
        house by Mies van der Rohe

        house by Walter Gropius

        Siedlung by Otto Haesler.

Holland
        house by J.J.P. Oud.

France
        College dormitory by Le Corbusier.

Nature of the Models: All the models, with one exception, will be constructed specially for the Exhibition.

The size of the models is approximately 3 ft. x 6 ft. The models will be constructed of "celon," wood, papier-mâché, glass, chrome, steel and marble. Particular care will be taken to provide for each model an attractive and appropriate setting consisting of trees, lawns, people and automobiles. As far as practicable, the interior planning will be revealed.

Both American and European models will be constructed by experts.

The models will be packed by professional packers. In unpacking and packing the models, each Museum is requested to employ professional packers.

RECOMMENDATIONS FOR INSTALLATIONS.

The space which should be allowed for the Exhibition is extremely flexible. In other words, the models may be so spaced to fill a large hall adequately or crowded together when the exhibition rooms are small. A minimum of 6 ft. should be allowed on each side of the model for proper circulation of visitors.

The weight of the model, including the weight of the packing case, is approximately 25 lbs.

The actual installation of the models need not be expensive. There is required only a stand for each model. This may be made economically of beaver board, or, if convenient, of wood, requiring no more than the services of a carpenter. In other words, the cost of installation depends on the elaborateness of the stands.

PHOTOGRAPHS AND RECOMMENDATIONS FOR

THEIR INSTALLATION.

Besides the model of each architect, there will be approximately five enlarged photographs which will illustrate his executed work. The photographs will be all of the same height - 35 inches. The width will depend on the proportion of the original photograph. It is strongly recommended that the photographs be placed in a frieze around the rooms, allowing about 2 ft. between each photograph. The space between the photographs will be used for the plan of the particular building represented. The photographs, which are mounted on plywood, will be hung in the same manner as paintings.

The total running feet of the Exhibition is approximately 500 ft.

The wall labels will be supplied by the Museum of Modern Art.

When accommodations are too small, omissions may be made in the case of both the models and the photographs without injuring the spirit of the Exhibition as a whole.

3.   CATALOGUE.

A specially prepared catalogue will be an important educational asset of the Exhibition.

The catalogue will contain 100 pages with 50 reproductions of the work of all the architects. The text will be a scholarly, historical and critical treatise on each architect, illustrated by material of historical as well as contemporary interest. In the case of the three German architects, the catalogue will contain the first three scholarly monographs written on these men in any language. The monographs will be prepared by Professor Henry-Russell Hitchcock, whose book "Modern Architecture" is the only scholarly work which has appeared on the subject to date.

Thus the catalogue will have a permanent value as a document in the history of architecture and will at the same time explain the aims and achievements of the greatest contemporary architects.

In order to determine a uniform price for the catalogue and also the number of editions, the Museum of Modern Art requests that each Museum advise the Secretary of the Exhibition the anticipated sale of catalogues in the respective Museums based on previous experience.

4.   LECTURES.

If the Museum desires to arrange for any number of lectures while the Exhibition is being held it may do so by communicating with the Secretary of the Exhibition at: Room 1007 Chatham Phenix Bank Bldg., Long Island City, New York.

At the present time two lecturers on Modern Architecture are available. Professor Henry-Russell Hitchcock, an authority on modern architecture, whose book, as mentioned above is the only scholarly work published on this subject to date, and Philip Johnson, graduate of Harvard University, who has studied modern architecture closely both in America and in Europe.

5.   INSURANCE.

The Museum of Modern Art advises the Museums that the models and photographs contained in the Architectural Exhibition are all thoroughly covered by insurance. It is not necessary for any Museum to take out insurance for any part of the Exhibition. The Museum of Modern Art requests that each Museum, when shipping the models to the next Museum, declares 10% of the value to the carrier. In the case of the models, this will be $200 each on a valuation of $2000 each, and on the photographs $2 on a valuation of $20 each.

Appendix 5

THE MUSEUM OF MODERN ART

Date: May 26, 1944

To:
Re: Bowman Brothers' Model of Lux Apartments
From: Mrs. Mock

_____

List of institutions at which International Exhibition of Modern Architecture was shown:

Dates		Institutions	Remarks
1932:	Mar 30 - Apr 22	Pennsylvania Museum of Art, Philadelphia, Pa.	no correspondence found
	May 2 - May 28	Wadsworth Atheneum, Hartford, Conn.	no correspondence found
	June 9 - July 8	Sears Roebuck, Chicago, Ill.	no mention in correspondence
	July 23 - Aug 30	Bullocks-Wilshire, Los Angeles,Cal.	no correspondence found
	Sept 15 - Oct 17	Buffalo Fine Arts Academy, Buffalo, N.Y.	no mention in correspondence
	Oct 27 - Dec 4	Cleveland Museum of Art, Cleveland, Ohio	in this show mentioned in check list in good condition
1933:	Feb 11 - Feb 28	Milwaukee Art Institute, Milwaukee, Wis.	in good condition: Feb 18
	Mar 17 - Apr 19	Cincinnati Art Museum, Cincinnati, Ohio	received
	Apr 29 - May 25	Rochester Memorial Art Gallery, Rochester, N.Y.	received
	June 5 - July 8	Worcester Art Museum, Worcester, Mass.	whatever arrived was in good condition
	July 22 - Aug 20	Currier Gallery of Art, Manchester, New Hampshire	no mention of exhibition
	Sept 1 - Sept 30	Toledo Museum of Art, Toledo,Ohio	no mention of any model
	Oct 11 - Nov 11	Fogg Art Museum, Cambridge,Mass.	no mention of model in correspondence
	Nov 17 - Dec 15	Dartmouth College, Hanover, N.H.	received at Dartmouth received at MMA Jan 5 '34

Complete Schedule

222

Photo Credits

Acknowledgements

For providing the initial support for the research for this document, I would like to thank Philip Johnson, Bernard Tschumi, Richard Oldenburg, Stuart Wrede and Rona Roob.

Throughout my research, Franz Schulze has been a source of excellent advice, broad general knowledge of the period and friendly support.

For giving their time to discuss their particular areas of expertise I'd like to thank Richard Pommer, Kenneth Frampton, Helen Searing, Martin Filler, Rosemarie Haag Bletter, Robert Wojtowicz, and Mary McLeod.

Rosemarie Bletter, Franz Schulze, Helen Searing, Rona Roob, Martin Filler and Brook Hodge also were kind enough to read the manuscript and for their comments and remarks I am grateful.

Production costs for this catalogue were supported in part by the Joseph E. Seagram & Sons, Inc.